Your First Gun

RODERICK WILLETT

Illustrations by Toby Buchan

Seeley, Service & Co.

LONDON

To Rita, who gave me
the encouragement and inspiration
to write this book.

First published in Great Britain in 1975 by
Seeley Service and Co,
196 Shaftesbury Avenue,
London WC2H 8JL

Copyright © 1975 by Roderick Willett
ISBN 0 85422 114 X

Set and printed in Great Britain by
Hollen Street Press Ltd at Slough

Contents

List of Illustrations

Chapter I

A plan for a shooting career

The acquisition of your first gun should be one of those rare moments in life which, despite the passage of years, is always recalled with pleasure and just a touch of the youthful excitement you experienced at the time. But, unhappily, the donor all too often fails to rise to the occasion through an inability to appreciate just how much care and attention ought to be devoted to it. Nothing is more frustrating to an aspiring young game shot than, having realized his ambition to possess a gun of his own, to find he can hit nothing with it! It is said the way to hell is paved with good intentions and to a boy or girl (girls can learn to shoot as well as boys) such a state of affairs is indeed a hell on earth, because no young person likes to make a laughing stock of himself, even only in his own eyes. Yet due to a combination of lack of thought and attention to elementary detail many young shots are launched on their shooting careers with a gun that is patently unsuitable in one or more respects. The aim of this book is to try and correct this state of affairs, so that not only does the novice start with every advantage but 'father' is soon made aware that his money has been well spent, and that, at the prices of guns today, is a matter of no small importance.

The purchase of a first gun should be considered in the context of a shooting career, not in isolation. Unless this is done guns will be bought at random and money may be wasted. The initial question is at what age a boy should start learning to handle and shoot with a shotgun. There are several factors which merit consideration in arriving at an answer. Most boys develop passing fancies, such as wanting to become an engine driver. So before buying an expensive gun it is wise to be as certain as you can that the desire to go shooting has come to stay. There is another aspect of this; some fathers, being keen shots themselves, automatically assume that their sons are going to be and are quite shattered when at a later date they are brought face to face with the reality of the situation, namely that the boy hasn't, and never has had, any enthusiasm for the sport at all, but has just been going along with father's wishes to keep him happy. I can recall at least one instance where relations between father and son became severely strained for a while, when the latter felt compelled to make it clear that he really did not want a pair of guns for his twenty-first birthday present. So in my view a parent should not be too eager to thrust a gun into his son's hands, but should play 'hard to get' for a while until he is satisfied that the interest is likely to be a continuing one.

I believe it is a mistake to purchase an airgun as a cheap and temporary expedient in these circumstances, just to keep the boy happy. The techniques of rifle and shotgun shooting are totally different from one another and in my experience if that of the former is learnt first it has a very inhibiting effect on mastery of the latter.

There are a number of restrictions in law on the use of shotguns by young people of which a parent should be aware so that he can decide how they affect the matter at issue, if at all. I have therefore set out the gist of these hereunder. However, I am not a lawyer and, in case of doubt on any point of law, I would stress most strongly the advisability of seeking a properly qualified opinion.

Under the law relating to Shotgun Certificates, it is illegal to sell, lend or give a shotgun to anyone who has not got a shotgun certificate; on no account may a shotgun be given to anybody under 15 years of age. The effect of this is that if, for example, a parent intends borrowing a shotgun off a neighbour for the use of his 13-year-old son in the school holidays, he, the parent, must have a valid shotgun certificate. However, the issue of shotgun certificates to young persons under 15 years of age is not debarred, though it will be at the discretion of the Chief Police Officer of the area to whom application is made. Unfortunately there is no stipulated or agreed minimum age at which a Chief Police Officer will issue such a certificate, so variations from place to place may well be found.

A shotgun certificate is NOT needed if:—

a. A shotgun is borrowed from the occupier of private premises, including land, and used thereon in his presence.

b. Someone else's shotgun is used on artificial targets at a place and time approved by the local Chief Police Officer, e.g. at an established shooting ground.

There are other exemptions, but they are not relevant to young shots. However, a number of clauses in the Firearms Acts 1937 and 1965, and the Airguns and Shotguns Act 1962 are of concern.

No one under 14 years of age may possess, purchase or acquire any firearm or ammunition, nor may he be lent any such weapon or ammunition. But he may:—

a. Possess and use firearms and ammunition as a member of an approved club, or when shooting in a shooting gallery where only air weapons or miniature rifles are available.

b. [This sub-para is not relevant to shotguns.]

c. Carry a firearm or ammunition under the instruction of another person over 21, who holds a valid shotgun or firearms certificate relating to the weapon or ammunition in question.

If a young person is under 15 years of age and has a shotgun certificate, he may have an assembled shotgun with him provided he is supervised by a person over 21 or the shotgun is carried in a gun cover securely fastened. When he is fifteen, or over, and has a shotgun certificate, he may be given a shotgun as a gift.

Until a young person is 17 years of age he may not purchase or hire any firearm or its ammunition. But on reaching this age, provided he has a shotgun certificate, he may possess, purchase, acquire and use a shotgun and ammunition subject only to the normal legal restrictions applicable in these respects to grown-ups.

So much then for the law. A factor which I have purposely kept till last is that of a young person's physical and mental capacity to use a shotgun. I know that young people today are alleged to mature both physically and mentally at an earlier age than did former generations and often exhibit impatience with restraints imposed on them by the latter. But a shotgun, even a small-bore one, is still a potentially lethal weapon if it is mis-handled. To be reasonably confident it won't be, a parent should be certain that not only is his offspring physically capable of handling a small-bore shotgun safely and competently, but that he is fully mentally alive to his responsibility so to handle it on all occasions. I believe therefore that as a general rule, 12 years of age is soon enough to be thinking in terms of a 'first gun', and 10 of handling a gun at all, and then only an unloaded one. It may in certain circumstances be justifiable to anticipate these ages by a year or thereabouts, but equally it could in others be prudent to delay making a start for a similar period.

A first gun, be it a .410 or 28-bore, the respective merits of which are argued in the next chapter, should be intended to last a young shot until he is about 16 years of age, i.e. for about four years. By that age a normally physically robust boy should be able to handle a 12-bore. But young shots are very supple and tend to 'shoot up' in their teens, only broadening out as they approach their twenties. Thus they do not really settle into a definite style of shooting, in which the fit of their gun in respect of bend and cast off becomes a matter of prime importance, until about 20-22 years of age. My advice therefore, regarding a first 12-bore at around 16 years old, would be to purchase an A.Y.A. standard boxlock ejector, which is a good cheap gun, and ought to give an aspiring shot a lot of excellent sport if the stock length is adjusted as necessary. There is one proviso to this; some people develop peculiarities of vision at an early age for which a stock merely of correct length is in-adequate, so if a stock with, for example, cast off substantially greater than the standard measurements is required, it should be provided. The reasons for this will be made clear in Chapter III.

Sometimes for reasons of economy, a 16-year-old may be required to make do with a 'family' 20-bore or 16-bore. This may be a source of mortification, but as will be explained in Chapter IV it ought not to be as much of a handicap as it is sometimes made out to be, and a young shot so equipped, who already displays the makings of a good shot, should be able to hold his own quite comfortably until the day arrives when he is taken to be measured and fitted for his coveted 12-bore. In my view his twenty-first birthday is quite time enough for a young shot to acquire a good gun, or pair of guns, with which he may hope to shoot for the rest of his life.

But now let us return to that 'first gun' of all and see what con-siderations in the light of all the above should affect its choice.

Chapter II

Selecting your first gun

To many of my generation one's first gun was a .410, and no question ever arose of it being anything else. This was, I believe, a thoroughly mistaken policy, which is still pursued too frequently today and leads to many young shots achieving unnecessarily disappointing results in their early shooting days, a time when they ought to be encouraged in every way to obtain the best possible results. From the point of view of performance, and by this I mean the pattern it throws, the popularity enjoyed by the .410 seems to me entirely unjustified. The patterns I have shot on the plate from various .410 barrels have been generally erratic from round to round in both quality and density, and the more choke there has been in a barrel the more marked these failings have been. In theory, with a 'Fourlong' cartridge and No. 7 shot, a .410 full choke barrel should enable a woodpigeon, or similar sized quarry, to be cleanly killed up to just over 30 yards' range, which, as one does not want youngsters falling into the bad habit of taking shots at excessive range, would be quite a reasonable limit. However, judging by patterns obtained on the plate, I doubt if such a result could be relied on in practice at a range of much over 20 yards, say a very maximum of 25. If No. 6 shot is used instead of No. 7 the pattern will be too thin anyway, so, instead of remedying matters, increasing the shot size will only worsen them. A maximum effective range of only 20-25 yards for small quarry, such as grey squirrels and woodpigeon, is very limiting indeed, and especially so if, when a boy is out with the 'grown ups', he is told he ought not to shoot any quarry at under 20 yards or he will be in danger of 'smashing' it. From observation in the field I am sure this limitation on a .410's performance is little appreciated and that it accounts for many of the failures to obtain clean kills at around the 30 yard mark, which are usually attributed to poor shooting, though the more likely cause is poor pattern. So although great fun can be had with a .410 shooting bolted rabbits at close quarters, or rats round a stack yard, or on certain other special occasions, it is not in my view a satisfactory weapon as a 'first gun' for a boy for general purpose shooting in the field.

There are various other drawbacks to .410s from a practical point of view. A shooting man will spend most of his life using a double barrelled, top lever gun. The sooner he can learn the drill of handling such a gun safely and competently, so that it becomes instinctive, the better. There is little objection in this respect to a single barrel, top lever gun, but few .410s of this kind are made. Quite a number of bolt-action single barrel .410s are marketed, which are simple, robust, inexpensive weapons. But all bolt-action shotguns tend to be muzzle heavy, especially when equipped with a short stock, as is necessary in the case of a boy's gun. Also the safety catch on the bolt is usually cumbersome to manipulate, and has to be put off before the gun is mounted. There are other types of single barrel .410, which have either hammer, or semi-hammerless actions, and in my view these should be avoided like the plague, not only because they can all too easily be fired inadvertently if the shooter's thumb slips off the spur of the hammer when cocking the weapon, but because a young shot has to learn a special safety drill in handling them, which will be no use when he graduates to a top lever, hammerless double barrelled gun.

But I can almost hear the gathering storm of protest over the question of over-gunning, so let us examine and dispose of this. Even a quite slenderly built boy of 12 should be able to handle a .410 with a 'Fourlong' load very comfortably, and no problem of this kind should arise with this bore. But the problem of under-gunning also merits attention. As has been stated above and will be elaborated in Chapter IV, the lethal capacity of a .410 is extremely limited, so much so in my opinion that it does not give a young shot a fair chance of putting into practice all those things that he is told to do when shooting live quarry, such as to make sure he does not cause unnecessary wounding by shooting at excessive range. Yet a combination of the small size of the shot load and the erratic patterning induced by the smallness of the bore make it almost impossible for him to put this excellent precept into effect if he also observes the similarly admirable one that quarry should not be shot at under 20 yards for fear of being smashed. This, I hope, has made it clear how too much emphasis on over-gunning can lead to a quite disastrous state of under-gunning, so let us see what the next largest gauge, the 28-bore, can offer.

From my experience of patterning them on the plate, 28-bores pattern, boring for boring, true to form, that is, an improved cylinder gives a 50% pattern, and a full choke one of 70%, or as near as makes no odds. This means we can place reasonable reliance on their theoretical performance being matched in practice. Thus if a standard 28-bore load of No. 7s is used in conjunction with an improved cylinder barrel we should expect to be able to kill a woodpigeon cleanly up to a range of 30 yards, and with a half-choke barrel up to 35 yards. My own observations in the field confirm this as being realistic, so let us see how the 28-bore meets any criticism of over-gunning.

A 28-bore standard load is $\frac{9}{16}$ ozs, i.e. $\frac{1}{8}$ oz more than the equivalent .410 'Fourlong' load. To keep the noticeable recoil equally acceptable, a rather heavier gun is required to handle this bigger load. Thus the weight of an ordinary $2\frac{1}{2}$ in chambered 28-bore is usually $4\frac{3}{4}$-5 lbs, whereas that of a comparable .410 would be 4-$4\frac{1}{2}$ lbs.

Over-gunning is considered almost exclusively in terms of un-acceptable recoil. But gun weight is also an important factor, because a gun that is too heavy for the user will mean that his arms quickly tire, as a result of which he fails to mount it correctly to his shoulder when taking his shots, and any ill-effects he is suffering from recoil are aggravated. I once spent a day shooting in the company of a boy aged 12 who was using a 16-bore. He was on the small side for his age and every time he pulled the trigger he visibly flinched. A 16-bore weighs about $5\frac{3}{4}$ lbs, and the standard load, which he was shooting, is $\frac{15}{16}$ ozs. This was a clear case of over-gunning in respect of both the recoil being excessive and the gun too heavy.

In my experience 12-year-olds are perfectly capable of shooting happily with a 28-bore and do not find the recoil excessive or the gun too heavy. They also achieve markedly more satisfactory results, especially when shooting at clays, than are obtainable with a .410, which is a positive encouragement to them and helps build their self-confidence which plays such a big part in the making of a competent shot. It should be clearly understood that because under-gunning makes the attainment of good results that much more difficult, and so prejudices the building of self-confidence it is a fault to be avoided almost as much as over-gunning.

I have had a 14-year-old of normal physique shooting away extremely contentedly at clays with a 2 in chambered 12-bore, which has the 'Two-Inch' load of $\frac{7}{8}$ ozs; but these guns are rather exceptional, being noted for their soft recoil. But the point at issue is that if a boy takes up shooting after 12 years old, or is big for his age at that juncture, the possibility of him having a 20-bore rather than a 28-bore should certainly be considered. However, for the majority of 12-year-olds a 28-bore should prove the right weapon for a first gun.

But whatever is finally decided upon, there are a number of other points which also ought to receive careful attention in selecting the actual gun. I have already indicated that a first gun should match in type as closely as possible that which will be used as a grown man. This means it should be a conventional double-barrelled, top lever operated weapon. However, having regard to the amount and type of shooting a boy is likely to enjoy, it is not in my view very material whether it is an ejector or non-ejector, and some may feel the latter is preferable on economic grounds. It is important that the stock should be properly shaped to meet the special needs of youthful physique. The mistake of many makers of proprietary small-bore guns is that they turn them out with a full man-sized stock, i.e. with one of standard length, namely $14\frac{3}{4}$ in, the butt of which is consequently too wide and too deep for slender shoulders, while the 'Hand' is often too massive for those with small hands to grip comfortably (see *Diagrams 1 & 2*). For quite a number of young shots a $12\frac{1}{2}$ in stock will prove quite long enough to begin with and the sole of the butt should be proportionately narrower and shallower, with the hand correspondingly slimmer.

Long barrels on a gun with a short stock spoil the symmetry of the weapon. They can also adversely affect its balance. Next to satisfactory shooting qualities, good balance is the most important characteristic of a gun. The term embraces a gun's dynamic handling qualities as well as merely its static point of balance,

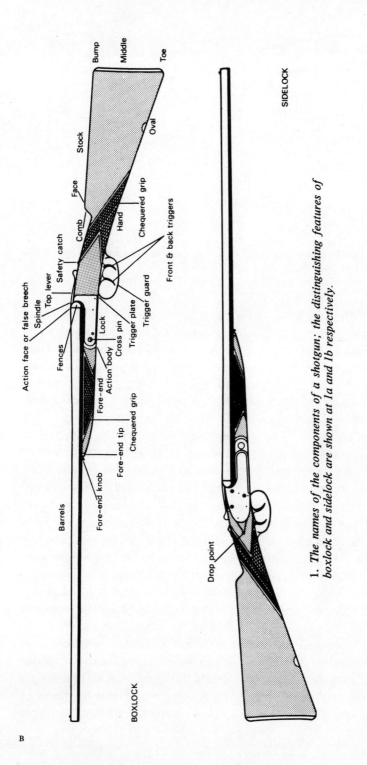

Action face or false breech
Spindle
Top lever
Safety catch
Fences
Fore-end
Action body
Lock
Cross pin
Trigger plate
Trigger guard
Chequered grip
Fore-end tip
Fore-end knob
Barrels

Bump
Middle
Toe
Stock
Oval
Face
Comb
Hand
Chequered grip
Front & back triggers

BOXLOCK

SIDELOCK

Drop point

1. *The names of the components of a shotgun; the distinguishing features of boxlock and sidelock are shown at 1a and 1b respectively.*

B

17

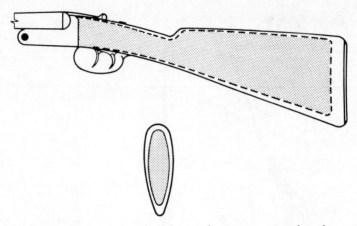

2. How the stock of a gun needs to be cut down to accommodate the smaller hands and slimmer shoulders of young shots.

which in all guns, however they handle, is normally in the region of the crosspin of the action (see *Diagram 1*). To ensure good, lively handling qualities, makers always try to concentrate the weight between the hands, as they describe it, that is approximately between the top of the fore-end, and the safety catch on the top of the hand of the stock. However, if you handle a 'well-balanced' gun, and then pick up one that feels like a weaver's beam, you will realize that it is correct distribution of weight, rather than mere concentration, which is the key to good balance. It will be readily understood therefore how a combination of a short stock and long barrels, where the former has been substantially reduced in length from that originally envisaged by the maker, can impair the balance of a gun. In my view 26- or 27-in barrels are the right length for a small-bore gun intended for a young shot, because they are in keeping with a short stock. Many older 28-bores were made, however, with 28-in barrels, and some even with 30-in ones. If such a gun was in the family's possession already and the barrels were in good order, subject to the advice of a reputable gunsmith, my inclination would be to have them cut down to 26 in. In doing so one would of course lose the original choke in the barrels. But nowadays this can be remedied by having choke swaged into the shortened barrels. Swaging is a comparatively new method of contriving choke in a barrel and consists simply of compressing the muzzle in a special machine, thus providing a

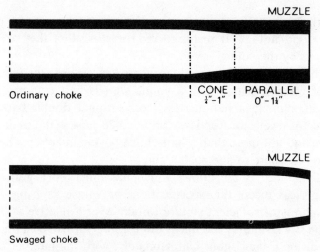

MUZZLE

Ordinary choke

!CONE ! PARALLEL !
¼"–1"   0"–1¼"

MUZZLE

Swaged choke

3. *Two methods of inserting choke in a gun barrel.*

choke with a cone but no parallel (see *Diagram 3*). It is therefore somewhat limited in application, a quarter-choke being about as much as can be obtained in a shortened barrel with sufficient metal in the barrel walls. It has been found in practice that swaged chokes usually give exceptionally good quality and regular patterns. As a young shot should be taught from the very beginning that a heavy choke in a game gun is a liability and not an asset, the reasons for which are fully explained in Chapter IV, having to shoot with only a quarter-choke in the left barrel of a 28-bore instead of a half-choke is no real handicap.

You may occasionally come across a single trigger 28-bore, which is likely to have been made as a bespoke gun of good, if not 'best', quality, and will therefore command a high price if it is in good order. My opinion is that the theoretical advantages claimed for single triggers are not material in practice, and unless a young shot either suffers from a hand injury which makes a single trigger obligatory, or is to inherit at a later date a pair of 'best' single trigger guns, it is better to stick to ordinary double triggers, which are essentially more robust, and less liable to mechanical failure.

I have once seen a bespoke 28-bore over and under, and Messrs Browning produce proprietary 'superposed shotguns', as they call them, in this gauge. But except for the boy who intends his main interest to lie with shooting clays rather than game, I do not believe they confer any material advantage in actual shooting,

19

while their normally greater cost and weight ($5\frac{3}{4}$-$6\frac{1}{4}$ lbs) may prove a real disadvantage. It seems to me therefore that they are best eschewed by the young novice.

We have now reached the stage where we can broadly define the kind of weapon with which a young shot is best equipped as a first gun, namely a hammerless, conventional double-barrelled, non-ejector or ejector, top lever actioned 28-bore with 26- or 27-in barrels, and not more than a half-choke boring in either. The next question is where to find such a gun.

Lucky indeed is the family which has inherited a gun which more or less meets this specification, or whose aspiring young sportsman is of sufficient stature to take over a relative's 20-bore with the stock suitably modified. But for many it will be a question of acquiring a 'new' gun. Unfortunately, with the number of old rook rifles converted into .410s, and the subsequent predominance of this gauge in the small-bore market, comparatively few 28-bores were made in the hey-day of British gunmaking around the beginning of this century. It is therefore quite a task to find secondhand ones, and is becoming more so with the growing realization in recent years of their superiority over the .410.

But secondhand 28-bores may be procured at auctions, through gunmakers or dealers, or advertisements in the sporting press. Prices vary enormously according to age, condition, maker's name, etc, from, say, one hundred to several hundred pounds. When a secondhand gun is bought from other than a reputable gunsmith or gun dealer, it is always advisable to obtain a second opinion as to its soundness, or after purchase it may be found necessary to spend a considerable sum on repairs to make it fit and safe to use. Where a gun is acquired from a private source always make it a condition of purchase that it be checked by a qualified gunsmith not only as to its general soundness, but also to confirm that it has passed nitro-proof, and is still in proof; it is illegal to offer for sale a gun which is not in proof, although this can quite easily be done unintentionally without criminal intent. It can be genuinely dangerous to shoot with a gun that is no longer in proof, however superficially sound it may appear.

Let us now turn to new guns. For some years Anglo-Spanish Imports have been marketing an excellent A.Y.A. double-barrelled, boxlock, non-ejector 28-bore with 27-in barrels at a price of under £110, as at the end of 1974. It has the great advantage that it is primarily intended as a gun for young shots. I have handled and shot these guns, and in my opinion they are excellent value for money; as a good parent is always primarily concerned with his children's safety, I would add that I would be very happy for a son of mine to shoot with one of them.

For those who have an innate prejudice against guns of other than British make, the only proprietary 28-bore produced in this country is that of Messrs Webley & Scott Ltd. It is a boxlock ejector, made to the same design as this firm's renowned 12-bore double-barrelled guns. It has 26-in barrels, but as it is intended more for the American than the home market, it is normally stocked for a man, not a boy, and is built on the heavy side, up to around $5\frac{1}{2}$ lbs in weight, in order to handle heavy American magnum loads. One of these guns costs approximately £450 at the time of writing. For an additional amount it is perfectly possible to have the stock modified by a gunsmith to suit a young shot, but in my view the question of their weight still counts too strongly against them, even if one is otherwise happy to sign a cheque for over £450.

For those prepared to pay for them, bespoke 28-bore boxlocks and sidelocks can still be obtained, built to the customer's order from leading British gunmakers, and very fine guns they are too; the price of the former will be around £800, and of the latter up to £4,000.

From the above prices it will be seen that those with modest purses do not have a wide field from which to choose. In fact their choice really lies between a reasonably priced secondhand gun and a new A.Y.A. My recommendation would be the latter for the following reasons. A well made, new gun is likely to give the better and more reliable service. If a new gun is purchased from a reputable gunsmith, he may well agree to make any necessary alterations to the stock without extra charge. It is in the interests of his own good name to see that the action is functioning properly, and in particular that the trigger pulls are satisfactory at the time of sale. If by mischance something goes wrong while the gun is still under warranty, it will be repaired by him free of charge.

But whatever the final selection of a first gun may be, I cannot stress too strongly the importance of it fitting the young shot for whom it is intended, so let us move on to the next chapter and see what this entails.

Chapter III

Gun fitting for young shots

Some people decry gun fitting and stigmatise it as a sort of gun-makers' confidence trick. I suppose that this is mainly because they fail to understand what it seeks to achieve. The aim of gun fitting is to make the muzzles point where the shooter is looking when the gun is correctly mounted to the shoulder. This means in effect that the centre line of the barrels must be made to coincide with the shooter's line of sight by 'bending' the stock in the vertical plane, and 'casting' it 'off' or 'on', depending whether a person is right- or left-handed, in the horizontal plane. But before either of these adjustments can be properly assessed, a stock must first be of the right length.

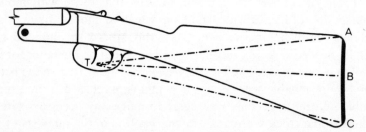

4. *Stock length is measured from the centre of the front trigger to the middle* (*BT*), *heel* (*AT*), *and toe* (*CT*) *of the butt; where only one measurement is given it is that of the line BT.*

Stock length is measured as shown in *Diagram 4*. Estimating the length needed is a job for an expert, such as a qualified shooting instructor, as it is vitally important that it should be correct. Some shooting men claim to be able to arrive at the answer by various homespun methods, such as placing the butt in the crook

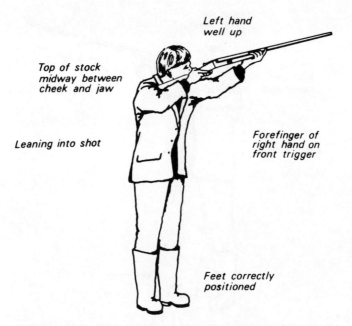

Left hand
well up

Top of stock
midway between
cheek and jaw

Leaning into shot

Forefinger of
right hand on
front trigger

Feet correctly
positioned

*5. When the stock is the right length the shooter is able to stand
and hold his gun correctly.*

of the elbow, and when the top joint of the forefinger can comfortably reach the front trigger, the stock is the right length. In my
own case, however, this produces a stock half an inch too short!
The only reliable way of assessing stock length is to use a try-gun
and adjust it until the butt comes comfortably and consistently to
the shoulder, as illustrated in *Diagram 5*. It will be seen in this
diagram that the shooter is able to reach the front trigger without
difficulty, the left hand is correctly positioned in the region of the
top of the fore-end, and the line of the top of the stock is resting
against his cheek mid-way between jawbone and cheekbone, as it
should be; his feet are correctly placed, and he is leaning slightly
forward into his shot. It will be noted that the boy is dressed for
shooting; this is important because, if he goes in shirt sleeves in
the summer holidays to be measured for a gun, and then sets out
to shoot around Christmas dressed in an anorak with a couple of
sweaters under it, he may well find his gun a good $\frac{1}{4}$ in too long in
the stock.

Too long a stock is something to be avoided at all costs in a

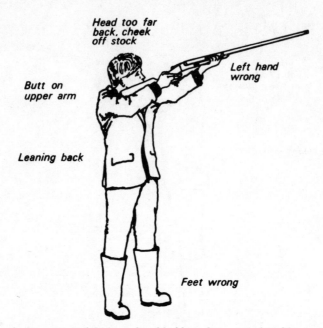

Head too far
back, cheek
off stock

Butt on
upper arm

Left hand
wrong

Leaning back

Feet wrong

6. *Some typical faults in hand holds and stance induced by too
long a stock.*

first gun. Salesmen in gun dealers sometimes recommend that a
stock be left on the long side, because a young person will soon
grow into it. However well-intentioned such advice may be, it is
thoroughly unsound. A stock that is significantly too long, and by
that I mean one exceeding the right length by a $\frac{1}{4}$ in or more, will
cause the state of affairs depicted in *Diagram 6*. In this it will be
noted that the shooter's left hand is too far back though his arm is
at almost full stretch; he can only barely reach the front trigger
with his right forefinger; the heel of the butt has caught on the
sleeve of his jacket, so that the butt is bedded against the point of
his shoulder and the top of his bicep, which, in the course of firing
only a few rounds, can result in painful bruising; he has had to
lean back in an endeavour to accommodate the butt in his shoulder
which, even if he had succeeded, would have meant the butt would
have bedded against bone rather than muscle with once again the
likelihood of bruising; and finally his cheek is off the stock which
means he is certain to miss his target anyway! Although not all
these faults may occur at every shot, for example the snagging of

the coat by the heel of the butt, some, such as the incorrect left hand hold, are unavoidable. I hope therefore that this is a sufficiently graphic illustration to show conclusively what a very real handicap too long a stock is, and how it can prevent a young shot from holding his gun properly, adopting the right stance and shooting successfully.

Of course if a stock has to be cut down to, say, $12\frac{1}{2}$ in for a boy aged 12, the time will come as he grows older when it ought to be lengthened. The consequences of shooting with too short a stock are not so disastrous as those with one too long, but they tend to be manifest in generally erratic performance, and possibly also a bruised second finger of the trigger hand, and so should be avoided. A competent gunsmith ought to be able to make a good job of lengthening a stock at comparatively small cost, especially if the piece of walnut originally cut from it is available. Also nowadays there are a number of excellent recoil pads, and plastic butt plates to be had which can be used instead of, or in addition to, wood to extend a butt. Even though the lengthening of a stock more than once may be considered to make it look unsightly, this should be regarded as a matter of only secondary importance to that of the young shot being able to handle his gun correctly right from the start, and thereafter. Unless this policy is adopted he will not be able to do justice to himself, his instructor, or the gun he has been given.

Mention was made in the last chapter that the stock of a boy's gun ought to be built on a smaller scale in certain respects than that of a man's, in order to meet the needs of his slighter physique (see *Diagram 2*). In this context the 'hand' of the A.Y.A. 28-bore is particularly to be commended; it is nice and slim so that a young person can take a firm grip, yet comfortably manipulate the safety catch and reach the forward trigger without having to shift his grip. The rather narrower butt also reduces the risk of bruising on the point of the shoulder as it can be more easily accommodated on the pectoral muscle.

Having obtained the correct length of stock, we can now turn to 'bend' and 'cast off'. The former provides the requisite elevation, and is measured as shown in *Diagram 7*. If a gun has too little bend, or in other words too straight a stock, it will shoot high; if it has too much bend, it will shoot low (see *Diagram 8*). It is sometimes argued that it is an advantage to have a gun which

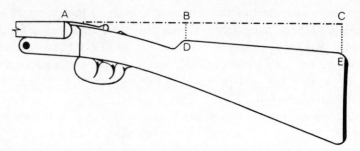

7. 'Bend' is the vertical distance at the comb (BD) and heel of a stock (CE) to a line in rearward extension of the top rib, ABC.

shoots high. Much of the sport enjoyed by a young shot will usually be at walked-up quarry, such as a pheasant rising from a root field, or a going away rabbit bolted from a tuft of grass in a pasture, so the disadvantage of a weapon which shoots low will be readily appreciated. Furthermore, in many of the shots which he will have to tackle later on at driven game, flighting duck or wood-pigeon, and other quarry it will be no less of a disadvantage. So although a gun should shoot where it is pointed, and it is funda-mentally wrong to build in a factor to compensate for poor marks-manship in one particular respect, it has been recognized that in game shooting it is on balance beneficial to have a gun which centres its pattern about 4 in above the mark. In guns for compe-tition clay pigeon shooting, a much greater margin is preferred but as the prevailing circumstances are totally different, the reasons for this need not concern the young game shot.

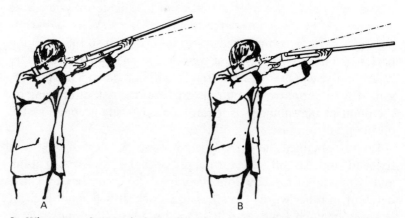

8. When a gun has too little bend on the stock it will shoot high, see 8a, and when too much, it will shoot low, see 8b.

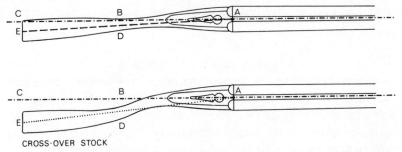

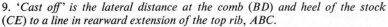

CROSS-OVER STOCK

9. *'Cast off' is the lateral distance at the comb (BD) and heel of the stock (CE) to a line in rearward extension of the top rib, ABC.*

As a rough guide, a tall young person with a long neck will need more bend on the stock than someone smaller with a short neck. But as with stock length, the best way to find out exactly what is required is to go to a qualified shooting coach, who with the aid of a try-gun will soon be able to advise you.

'Cast off' is the lateral adjustment to the stock necessary to make the centre line of the barrels, normally the top rib, coincide with the shooter's line of sight. It is measured as shown in *Diagram 9*. If a gun has insufficient cast off on the stock, it will shoot to the left of the mark, and if too much, to the right of the mark, as

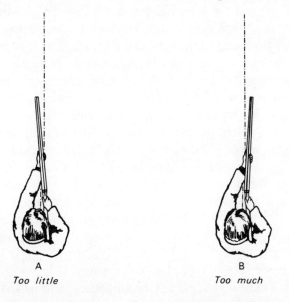

A
Too little

B
Too much

10. *When there is insufficient cast off on a stock, the gun will shoot to the left of the mark, see 10a, and when too much, to the right of the mark, see 10b.*

27

illustrated in *Diagram 10*. For a left-handed person a stock is 'cast on'.

Generally speaking exactly the right cast off on a first gun for a young shot is of less importance than it will be on the gun he will acquire when grown up. In case this smacks of heresy, let me give the reasons. Minor discrepancies in cast off do not become significant till over a range of 30 yards, though at 40 yards they may cause a target to be missed completely. The slender build of a young shot means that the horizontal displacement of the eye in relation to the place at his shoulder where the stock beds home is substantially smaller than it will be when he has grown up and broadened out. Young people are very supple, and until their muscles have fully developed and set, they do not really settle down into a definite, consistent style of shooting. So it is quite possible that a boy of 12-14 years of age will shoot successfully with a straight-stocked gun, yet by the time he has reached 21 will genuinely need more than average cast off. However, the cast off required by a young shot should not be just left to chance, but checked at the same time as he is measured for length and bend, for though the majority may require little or none, there are exceptions to this, as to every rule.

The above are the principal details we have to consider in gun fitting. Nobody will ever be able to shoot his best unless he has a gun which fits him, and though bend and cast off may be matters of less significance, this applies with no less force in the case of young shots than in that of adults. Unless a gun can be mounted correctly, and consistently so, to the shoulder good results in shooting cannot be expected. To try and make good any shortcomings in the fit of his gun a boy will inevitably be driven to attempt to fit himself to it. Thus, for example, if he finds the stock does not readily come up to meet his cheek, he may start to bob his head down to meet it, which is a common cause of missing, and a fault difficult to eradicate once it has become habitual, though unfortunately only one of many for which a badly fitting gun can be responsible. What might be called 'body fitting' is not a satisfactory substitute for gun fitting. As will be explained in Chapter VI, good style and technique are just as crucial to the mastery of game shooting as they are to that of golf, cricket, or any other game or sport. Good performers are found occasionally who appear to flout this convention, but in my view they are good in spite of so doing, not because they do so.

I hope, therefore, that I have managed to convince the reader that gun fitting is not just a lot of fuss about nothing, but something genuinely deserving of proper attention and understanding by those who wish to gain the maximum pleasure from their sport and help aspiring young shots to do the same.

Chapter IV

Elementary gun know-how

Many British shooting men of mine and former generations have made a virtue of ignorance of the technicalities of shotgun and cartridge, so much so that some do not even know the difference between a boxlock and a sidelock. This may not have mattered much in the days when one could rely on one's gunmaker to take care of, or advise on, such details. But now the provincial gunmaker and gunsmith has to a great extent either vanished or been replaced by the gun dealer who trades also in fishing tackle, sports kit, bicycles and so on, and who is probably better able to advise on tennis rackets or wet suits for water-skiing than on guns and cartridges. So unless one can avail oneself of the services of one of the few remaining genuine provincial gunmakers or those of a leading London, Birmingham or Edinburgh maker, one has to look to one's own resources. Lack of an elementary knowledge carries its penalties. Someone once showed me a 'sidelock' he believed he had picked up very cheaply. On inspection it proved to be a boxlock with ornamental side plates, as sometimes fitted to these guns. As such, at the price he had paid, it was far from a bargain. An old gentleman of my acquaintance had a 12-bore which he was convinced was a valuable gun, and had insured it accordingly. When he died and the gun was valued, it transpired that it was a very ordinary weapon, not worth a quarter of what he had imagined, and consequently had been grossly over-insured for years. So the young shot of today will unquestionably benefit from acquiring a sound elementary knowledge of shotguns and their ballistics. It can save him wasting his hard-earned pennies and can also be of practical value in assisting him to obtain good results in the field.

The gun most widely used for shooting in the British Isles is the double-barrelled (side-by-side), hammerless ejector, sidelock or boxlock. In Scotland, though comparatively rarely in England, Dickson 'Round Action' guns will also be seen. Repeating and automatic weapons are seldom used because they have been found unsuitable, largely on grounds of safety.

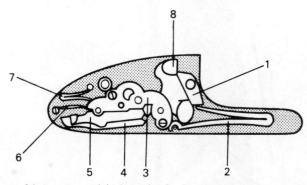

11. *A typical bar action sidelock in the fired position; the names of the parts are:— 1 The Tumbler Stop; 2 The Main Spring; 3 The Bridle; 4 The Sear; 5 The Intercepting Safety; 6 The Intercepting Safety Spring; 7 The Sear Spring; 8 The Tumbler.*

In the days of flint and percussion lock muzzle loaders, all guns were sidelocks. The early breech-loading hammer guns followed the fashion. From these in about 1870 was developed the hammer-less sidelock action, in which the hammer was enclosed in the lock and renamed a 'tumbler'. A typical modern bar action sidelock is shown in *Diagram 11*. If this is looked at in conjunction with *Diagram 1*, it will be seen that there is one lock for each barrel and the working parts of each are carried on a separate plate. The main portion of each lock mechanism fits into a space cut in the head of the stock behind the face of the action and only the V-mainspring has to be accommodated in the bar of the action. As there remains just the Purdey double-bolt, which we will deal with in a moment, to be built into this part of the action, it permits the bar to be given a very strong cross-section. The intercepting safety is of interest and one will be found in all good sidelocks. It should be clearly understood by young shots that the safety catch on a gun only locks the triggers, preventing them being pulled in-

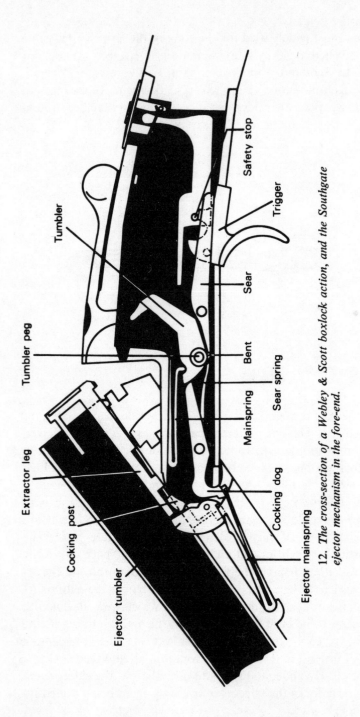

Tumbler

Tumbler peg

Extractor leg

Cocking post

Ejector tumbler

Ejector mainspring

Safety stop

Trigger

Sear

Bent

Mainspring

Sear spring

Cocking dog

12. *The cross-section of a Webley & Scott boxlock action, and the Southgate ejector mechanism in the fore-end.*

advertently. In a lock without an intercepting safety it is possible that if it is severely jolted the sear nose will slip out of the bent, and then, despite the safety catch being applied, the tumbler will be impelled forward by the mainspring and fire the cartridge. An intercepting safety device is designed so that in this eventuality the tumbler is caught and held on its way forward in a sort of half-cock position, thus preventing the firing of the cartridge. The best of these mechanisms are as near foolproof as human ingenuity can make them, but anything mechanical is fallible, and a gun with intercepting safeties should be treated with no less respect and regard for safety routine than one without.

In 1875 Messrs Anson & Deeley produced their famous boxlock action. Because it is of simpler design than a sidelock, it is also cheaper and easier to make, and is therefore used in less expensive guns. One of the best modern versions of this action is that of Messers Webley & Scott, a cross-section of which is shown in *Diagram 12*. As will be seen, both locks are housed mainly in the bar of the action, and the two tumblers rotate about a single peg which passes right through the action body. The Purdey double-bolt is also accommodated in the bar, as with the sidelock. So it will be realized that it is not possible to design the cross-section of the bar of a boxlock to be as strong as that of a sidelock. It will also be seen that the mainspring is less massive, and because lack of space prohibits the working parts being sited quite as advantageously from a technical viewpoint, a boxlock is slightly less mechanically efficient than a sidelock. For the same reason there is usually no intercepting safety incorporated, so a boxlock is that much less safe. But as far as a young shooter is concerned, a good quality boxlock should give him years of reliable service if he looks after it properly, and unless he abuses it by firing loads in excess of those for which it has passed proof, should stand up to ordinary hard shooting in the field just as well as a sidelock. It is worth remembering that despite the passage of a hundred years, the Anson & Deeley design has remained virtually unchanged, and is still the most widely used in gunmaking today. This would not have been so had its merits not been found sufficient to discount the advantages of the sidelock.

The barrels of a modern shotgun are made of steel. The various parts are depicted in *Diagram 13*. I have come across one or two examples of 28-bores with Damascus barrels, i.e. of iron and steel

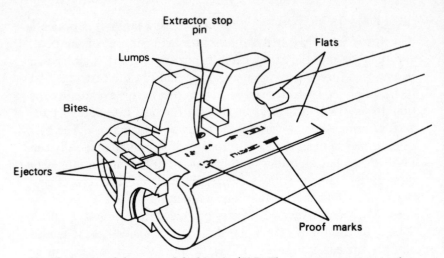

13. *The names of the parts of the barrels.* (*N.B. The extractor stop pin is often in the forward lump.*)

twisted and welded together. But as such a gun will certainly be old and possibly not in pristine condition, and even the best Damascus barrels were liable to have flaws in them, I would not recommend the acquisition of one as a first gun.

Shotgun barrels are brazed together at the breech end in one of various ways. On the underside of the chambers are the 'flats', which bed down on the corresponding flats on top of the bar of the action when the gun is closed. Closure is effected by means of the Purdey double-bolt, which slots into the bites in the lumps. As shown in *Diagram 14*, the forward bolt 'B' fits into the bite 'D' in the forward lump, and acts more in the nature of a guide; it is the rear bolt 'C' that must be a really accurate fit and bear down hard

14. *The Purdey double-bolt.*

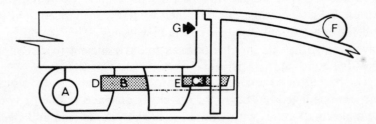

on the bite 'E' in the rear lump to give a satisfactory closure. If the workmanship in this respect is sound, there is no need for a top extension at 'G', as is found in some guns. 'A' is the crosspin of the action about which the hook in the forward lump turns; this may be an actual pin, as in all 'best' guns, or be cut out of the steel of the knuckle. 'F' is the top lever, which actuates the Purdey double-bolt. Finally the barrels are prevented from falling off the crosspin by placing the fore-end in position, which is attached to them by a snap-catch which fits into the 'loop' on their underside. In the case of an ejector gun, the mechanism is housed in the fore-end; the type most commonly used in modern British guns is the Southgate, or a variation of it; it consists in effect of two small locks which operate on the over-centre principle, like the blade of a penknife, each tumbler being timed so that it goes over-centre and strikes its extractor leg as the breech has opened sufficiently to allow the empty cartridge case to be 'shot' clear of the action face.

A word about the Dickson 'Round Action'; this is a superb action which combines great strength with mechanical efficiency. It is entirely different in design from either boxlock or sidelock; both locks are carried on a vertical steel plate affixed to the trigger plate; a further point of difference is that the ejectors are housed in the body of the action. If the opportunity of acquiring a 'Round Action' arises, jump at it, if you can afford it!

A point that may need attention, particularly in a new first gun, is the trigger pulls, which can sometimes be too heavy and sluggish. They should be adjusted so that they are nice and crisp, with the pull of the front trigger being about $3\frac{1}{2}$ lbs and that of the rear one 4 lbs or a trifle more, owing to the greater leverage obtained.

Let us now move on to the cartridge. The components of a typical modern British game cartridge are shown in *Diagram 15*. Leading cartridge makers in this country have in recent years gone to a great deal of trouble to ensure that their wares give satisfactory and consistent round to round ballistics, which in turn means that if the gun in which they are used is in good order, they will give high quality, uniform patterns. British cartridges have attained an excellent standard of reliability in both their functioning and per-formance. I mention this because if we are shooting badly, we all, young and old, tend to blame the cartridge, and wonder if a differ-ent brand, a faster load, or larger shot might not put matters to rights. The short answer is almost certainly 'NO', and whatever

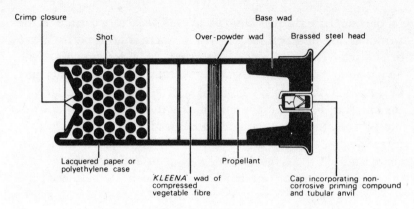

Crimp closure

Shot

Over-powder wad

Base wad

Brassed steel head

Lacquered paper or polyethylene case

KLEENA wad of compressed vegetable fibre

Propellant

Cap incorporating non-corrosive priming compound and tubular anvil

15. *The components of an 'Eley' game cartridge.*

the fault may be, it is far more probable that it lies with our gun or our shooting, and the best person to rectify it is a qualified instructor. As will be explained in a moment, heavier, faster loads, or larger shot are more likely to exacerbate the condition they are intended to cure. As regards foreign cartridges to which some people hopefully turn, some are good, others less so, and none in my view has any material advantage to offer. I believe the young shot cannot do better than pin his faith on the standard load British game cartridge if he wishes to obtain the best results in the field that his own abilities will allow.

When a cartridge is fired the priming compound in the cap ignites the propellant, which is immediately converted into gases; the pressure generated by the expansion of these drives the shot charge up the barrel and onwards to the target. Game guns of all bores with $2\frac{1}{2}$ in chambers which handle the standard load are proved for a maximum mean service pressure of 3 tons per square inch (t.s.i.). With good cartridges round to round pressures may vary by up to about .25 t.s.i. above and below a datum point, so makers usually aim for a mean service pressure of around 2.6 t.s.i. in their cartridges.

With rifles velocity is always evaluated in terms of muzzle velocity. But with shotguns this is impracticable because to compensate for the more rapid loss of velocity by smaller shot after leaving the bore they have to be sent on their way with a slightly higher muzzle velocity than their larger brethren. However, a common denominator has been found in the mean velocity over the first 20 yards of their trajectory; this is known as the observed velocity. Standard velocity, i.e. that of a standard load, is an observed velocity of 1070 feet per second (f.p.s.) for all shot sizes, and high velocity (H.V.) one of 1120 f.p.s. Good penetration, i.e. the lethal effectiveness of individual pellets, is dependent on adequate velocity. However, it should be remembered that high pressures and high velocities tend to disperse patterns and it has been found with velocities much in excess of 1120 f.p.s. not only do patterns become so dispersed, or 'blown', as to be ineffective, but recoil also becomes quite unacceptable.

Old timers often used to judge the excellence of a cartridge by the noticeability of its recoil. But advances in modern powders have made such crude methods of assessment entirely obsolete, and provided its ballistics are otherwise up to standard, it is the lack of noticeable recoil that should be considered the hallmark of a good modern cartridge. This of course depends on a gun of appropriate weight being used; as a rough guide, it has been found that a 1 oz load requires a gun of 6 lbs to keep noticeable recoil within acceptable limits, and lighter or heavier loads should be used with proportionately lighter or heavier guns.

Some established shot loads, together with a note of the guns that handle them, are given in Table 1, below.

THE NUMBER OF PELLETS IN DIFFERENT CHARGES OF SHOT

SIZE OF SHOT	a	a	b	c	d	e	f	g	h
	$1\frac{1}{16}$	1	$\frac{15}{16}$	$\frac{7}{8}$	$\frac{13}{16}$	$\frac{5}{8}$	$\frac{9}{16}$	$\frac{7}{16}$	$\frac{5}{16}$
3	149	140	–	–	–	–	–	–	–
4	181	170	159	149	138	106	96	–	–
5	234	220	206	193	179	138	124	96	–
6	287	270	253	236	219	169	152	118	84
7	361	340	319	298	276	212	191	149	106
8	478	450	422	394	366	281	253	196	140
9	616	580	544	508	471	363	326	254	184

Load in ounces

NOTES a. These are both 12-bore game loads, $1\frac{1}{16}$ ozs being the standard load.

b. This is the standard 16-bore load.

c. This is the 2 in chambered 12-bore load.

d. This is the standard 20-bore load.

e. This is the magnum 3 in .410 load, included for purposes of comparison.

f. This is the standard 28-bore load.

g. This is the 2½ in .410 load.

h. This is the 2 in .410 load.

I have purposely refrained so far from mentioning magnums and magnum loads because such guns with their heavily choked barrels are, in my opinion, unsuitable for general game and rough shooting in this country, and as a first gun merely encourage a novice to take shots at quarry that is really out of range. Further, to use a small-bore magnum to handle a load which a game gun of larger bore will handle more efficiently is unsound practice. When he has learnt to shoot reasonably successfully with an ordinary game gun within the normally accepted sporting limits, say some time after he has acquired his first 12-bore, will be quite time enough to introduce the magnum concept, and the realities of effective shooting with heavy loads and large shot at longer ranges. However, I have included the 3 in .410 magnum load in the above Table to show what very little advantage it offers in terms of extra pellets over the standard 28-bore load.

If there was a chance of some quarry, say a wounded rabbit, turning at bay and doing its pursuers and their dogs a serious mischief, greater interest might be taken in the patterns shot by guns instead of leaving this crucial matter largely in the lap of the gods. If somebody attempted to take an unzeroed rifle, or one with inadequate ballistics, to the hill to shoot a stag, his host would quite rightly stop him. Yet there are today novice shots of all ages taking the field with gun and cartridge of which they have never seen the patterns on the plate, and the lethal adequacy of which is extremely doubtful. To do this as a 'gun' is no less an abuse of the code of good sportsmanship than as a 'rifle'.

To be lethally effective a pattern must have sufficient pellets to ensure a strike by at least one on a vulnerable part, e.g. the head, and each pellet must have sufficient striking energy to deliver a lethal blow on such a part. The density of a pattern, i.e. the numerical sufficiency of the pellets, is assessed in terms of the number placed in a 30 in circle at any given range. With guns of 20-bore and larger, performance is normally compared at 40 yards, which has come to be accepted as the limit at which shots ought to be taken in the field. The maximum effective range of a game gun is regarded as 45 yards, because beyond this point patterns of small shot, i.e. 5s, 6s and 7s, deteriorate very rapidly in both density and quality. However, with the smaller bores, such as the 28-bore and .410, there are substantially fewer pellets in the charge, and the equivalent ranges should be taken as 30 and 35 yards respectively.

The percentage of the shot charge placed in the 30 in circle at various ranges by different choke borings is shown in Table 2 below.

BORING OF GUN	Range in yards					
	20	25	30	35	40	45
True Cylinder	90	73	60	49	40	33
Imp Cylinder	96	84	72	60	50	41
¼ Choke	98	89	77	65	55	46
½ Choke	100	96	83	71	60	50
¾ Choke	100	100	91	77	65	60
Full Choke	100	100	100	84	70	59

A common misapprehension is that the smaller the bore, the smaller the overall spread of the pattern. This is a complete fallacy; the diameter of the pattern shot by all bores with an equal degree of choke in the barrel is just about the same. The essential difference between a pattern shot by a 12-bore with a given shot size, and that by a 28-bore with the same shot size lies in the greater number of pellets the former will place within the same circumference.

The individual striking energies of pellets in foot-pounds for different shot sizes at various ranges with standard velocity cartridges are given in Table 3 below.

SIZE OF SHOT	Range in yards				
	20	30	35	40	45
4	4.66	3.52	3.04	2.65	2.28
5	3.51	2.59	2.22	1.89	1.61
6	2.79	2.01	1.71	1.43	1.21
7	2.17	1.51	1.26	1.05	0.86
8	1.57	1.06	0.86	0.70	0.56
9	1.19	0.77	0.62	0.49	0.39

Let us now see what the requirements are in terms of lethal pattern, i.e. of density and striking energy, for our various quarry. These have been estimated chiefly from empirical observations in the field combined with experiments on artificial targets and dead game, supported by scientific calculations. The patterns shot by well regulated guns may vary from round to round in density by 5-10%, or more in weapons of poorer quality; also even in the best quality patterns the pellets will not be evenly distributed over the 30 in circle, but gaps of significant size will appear here and there. Another factor is that the larger the quarry, the heavier the flesh and bone, so that not only are the vital parts better protected but comprise a smaller proportion of the total body area. Estimating necessary pattern densities is not, therefore, just a simple mathematical calculation.

It has come to be recognized that the following minimum pattern densities in the 30 in circle are needed to ensure a clean kill for the quarry shown:—

Snipe	290
Golden Plover	220
Woodcock and Teal	145
Partridge and Woodpigeon	130
Grouse	120
Pheasant, Blackcock and Mallard	100
Capercaillie and Goose	70
Rabbit	100
Hare	70

The corresponding minimum lethal striking energies required by individual pellets are:—

Snipe, Golden Plover, etc	0.50 ft lbs
Woodcock, Teal, Patridge, Woodpigeon, Grouse, etc	0.85 ft lbs
Pheasant, Blackcock, Mallard, etc	1.00 ft lbs
Capercaillie, Goose, etc	1.50 ft lbs
Rabbit	1.00 ft lbs
Hare	1.50 ft lbs

With the aid of these data we can now find out how we can use our 28-bore standard load to best effect. Let us assume that we have an improved cylinder boring in the right barrel and a ½ choke in the left. If we use No. 7 shot, Table 3 shows us that our pellets will have a striking energy of over 1 ft lb up to a range of 40 yards.

Table 1 tells us that the total number of pellets in the standard load is 191. By using Table 2 we can calculate that we should be able to anticipate the following pattern densities at the ranges shown:—

BARREL		Range in yards				
(With No. 7 Shot)	20	25	30	35	40	45
Right, Imp Cyl.	183	160	137	115	95	64
Left, ½ Choke	191	183	158	135	115	95

This reveals that we should be able to kill woodcock, teal, partridges, woodpigeon and grouse up to a range of 30 yards with our right barrel and 35 yards with our left; similarly we should be able to deal with rabbits up to 35 and 40 yards respectively. If we wish to shoot snipe, we shall have to use No. 9 shot and restrict our shooting to under 28 yards, which in practice will be very limiting. If we are invited to shoot hares we should use a larger shot size than No. 7; No. 6s will give us adequate pattern density and striking energy up to 30 yards with both barrels, and shots at hares should not be attempted at longer ranges by inexperienced shooters.

Let us now compare this with what a .410 with similar borings can appear to offer. Table 1 tells us that with 7s the number of pellets in the 2½ in .410 load is 149. By using Table 2 again we should find that we have the following densities:—

BARREL		Range in yards				
(With No. 7 Shot)	20	25	30	35	40	45
Right, Imp Cyl.	144	126	107	90	74	61
Left, ½ Choke	149	144	124	106	90	74
Full Choke	149	149	149	126	105	89

The above data show that the .410 improved cylinder barrel has an insufficiently dense pattern to be sure of killing a bird the size of a woodpigeon at 25 yards and beyond, although the ½ choke barrel should permit us to do so up to almost 30 yards. Even using a full choke barrel will only extend the range to just under 35 yards. However, substituting No. 8 shot will improve matters, as the figures below indicate:—

BARREL			*Range in yards*			
(*With No. 8 Shot*)	20	25	30	35	40	45
Right, Imp Cyl.	188	164	141	117	Insufficient	
Left, ½ Choke	196	188	162	139	Striking Energy	

The above shows that No. 8 shot should permit a .410 to shoot lethal patterns for quarry the size of a woodpigeon with an improved cylinder barrel up to 30 yards, and with a ½ choke up to 35 yards, beyond which these small pellets run out of necessary striking energy. But unfortunately in practice I have yet to find a .410 barrel that patterns up to par, so to speak, and this is a finding I have had confirmed by others who have tested these guns. So the maximum effective range of a .410 can in practice only be considered as 25 yards.

But the really important factor that emerges from our investigations above is the need to use a small shot size, No. 7s in the case of the 28-bore, and No 8s in that of the .410, in order to obtain the best results from these little guns. I cannot emphasize too strongly that it is folly to have surplus pellet striking energy, i.e. too large a shot size, where this is at the expense of adequate pattern density, because weak patterns will only wound instead of killing cleanly.

For comparison, a pattern shot by a .410, 3 in magnum load of No 6s at 30 yards with a full choke barrel is shown in *Diagram 16a*, while in *Diagram 16b* is shown the pattern shot by a 28-bore standard load of No. 7 shot at the same range using an improved cylinder barrel; in *Diagram 16c* is the pattern shot by a 12-bore improved cylinder barrel at 40 yards with a standard load of No. 6s. The two points of particular interest are the weakness of the .410 pattern which should in theory have matched in density that of the 28-bore and how well the 28-bore pattern at 30 yards compares in quality with that of the 12-bore at 40 yards. It also confirms how truly effective a 28-bore can be at 30 yards if used in conjunction with an appropriate shot size.

A shotgun today is a valuable weapon, and if it is to retain its value must be properly cared for after firing and when not in use.

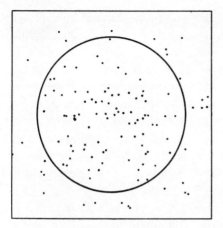

16a. *The pattern of a .410 x 3 in magnum load of ⅝ ozs of No. 6 shot at 30 yards range using a full choke barrel. There are only 94 pellets in the 30 in circle instead of an anticipated 135. This is typical of the substandard and erratic patterns obtained with heavily choked .410's, and especially with magnum loads.*

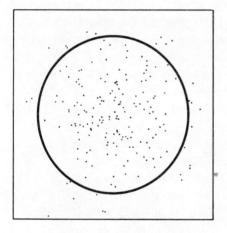

16b. *The pattern of a standard 28-bore load of 9/16 ozs of No. 7 shot at 30 yards using an improved cylinder barrel. There are 144 pellets in the 30 in circle instead of an anticipated 136, well illustrating the better quality and more reliable patterns obtained with a 28-bore in conjunction with the standard load, and 'game' borings.*

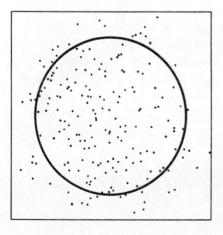

16c. *The pattern of a standard 12-bore load of 1 1/16 ozs of No. 6 shot at 40 yards using an improved cylinder barrel. There are 146 pellets in the 30 in circle instead of an anticipated 144. This is a good quality pattern. It is noteworthy how favourably the 28-bore pattern (Figure 16b) at 30 yards with No. 7 shot compares.*

Modern cleaner/lubricants in aerosol packs have taken all the hard work out of routine cleaning after firing. First the gun should be taken down into its three principal components by removing the fore-end, and then opening the breech and unhitching the barrels from the crosspin. A plain, wooden-topped kitchen table on which to place them is ideal, as the spilling of a few drops of oil will not matter. The cleaner/lubricant should be sprayed down each barrel, assuming both have been fired, from the breech end. The barrels should then be left flat on the table for ten minutes or so. The stock and fore-end can now be wiped over with a dry cloth, and any mud in the chequering brushed out with an old toothbrush. After shooting in the rain, I always like to wipe off any moisture with a cloth, a piece of old flannel shirt will serve excellently, as I am dismantling the gun; water will almost certainly have seeped under the fore-end and penetrated around the knuckle, both of which areas should be thoroughly dried; the channels on either side of the top rib need careful drying, and if after a preliminary wipe with a cloth, the edge of a piece of blotting paper is run down each, it should remove any residual damp. After the stock and fore-end have been cleaned and dried, the metal parts should be wiped over with an oily rag, and just a touch of '3-in-One', or some other penetrating oil, applied to the moving parts, such as the Purdey double-bolt, the top lever, etc; the tip of a pigeon's wing feather dipped in a little oil should enable the nooks and crannies to be reached without difficulty. Turning once more to the barrels, I usually pull them through with a bristle brush behind which is a wad of 4 x 2 flannelette sufficiently big to fit the bore reasonably tightly. After each barrel has been pulled through twice with this combination, the bores should be inspected, and if there is no sign of fouling, especially just in front of the chamber or immediately behind the choke, the barrels can be oiled up with an oily mop lightly impregnated with the cleaner/lubricant. If, however, on our inspection of the bores, white streaks of leading are seen, they will need to be tackled with a phosphor bronze brush to which the cleaner/lubricant has been liberally applied; this brush won't damage the bores, so it can be used as vigorously as need be, until the leading has been scrubbed out. When this has been achieved, the bores should be wiped clean and then oiled up as already described. If, after shooting in the rain, water is seen to have got behind the extractors, these can easily be removed by unscrewing the stop pin in the forward lump, but it is important to use a screwdriver that fits or you will burr the head. When you have dried out the tunnel in which the extractor legs move, for which a pipe cleaner is useful, wipe them over with the oily rag and replace them together with the screw in the forward lump.

There are several ways in which the wood of the stock and fore-end can be treated to keep it in good order. I still find buffing in a little boiled linseed oil with the heel of the hand is the best. But for those to whom this may seem rather old-fashioned, a good wax furniture polish will serve very well, as will a rub with a silicone-impregnated cloth.

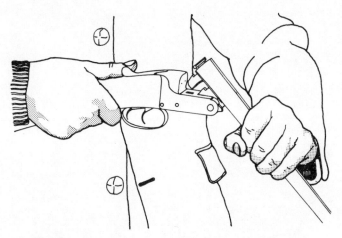

17. *The correct way to reassemble the barrels and action.*

When all this has been done, the gun should either be re-assembled and placed in a gun cabinet, or the fore-end replaced on the barrels, and these, together with the stock, returned to their gun case. However, if a gun is stiff to reassemble, as some ejectors can be, it is important not to damage the lumps or flats of the action. To avoid this the stock should be held in the right hand with the butt pressed against the body by the right forearm (see *Diagram 17*) while the small of the butt is gripped by the right hand, and the top lever is pushed over with the thumb. The barrels should be held by the left hand close up to the breech, and the hook in the forward lump placed over the crosspin. If a steady pull is maintained against the crosspin as the breech is closed, there should be no trouble in effecting this smoothly. It then only remains to snap the fore-end into position.

Even though a gun be well maintained and suffer no obvious damage in the course of a season, an annual overhaul by a qualified gunsmith is a sound policy, if only to confirm that all is as well as it appears to be, and our young shot really does deserve a pat on the back for the way he has looked after his gun.

Chapter V

Safe gun handling

The first aim of every young man who goes game shooting should be to earn himself a reputation as a safe shot. If he can complement this with one as a first class marksman, good luck to him; it will make him doubly welcome as a guest gun. But he should clearly understand from the moment he first carries a gun in the field that safety takes precedence over marksmanship as the greatest virtue of them all, and never allow himself to forget it throughout his shooting career.

There are two sides to safety in the field. The first is to make sure you shoot with a mechanically safe and sound gun; the second to know how to handle it safely. The advisability of sending a gun for an annual overhaul was mentioned in the last chapter. A well maintained gun is generally a safe gun, just as is a well looked-after car. Also just as the price you pay for a car will normally reflect its quality, age and mechanical condition, so will what you pay for a gun.

Some shooting people assert that they can see no point in paying the high price of a 'best' gun, because you are only paying for a 'name'. This is nonsense. As the description implies these guns are made from genuinely best quality materials, by the finest craftsmen, their finish is superb and likewise their functioning, and their shooting performance will be as consistent with specification as it is possible to make it; further they are backed by a first rate maintenance and repair service. So in my opinion a 'best' gun warrants its high price, and fortunate indeed is he who as a young shot can shoot with one. But the majority of us will not be so fortunate, and have to be content with a less expensive, but still reputable, weapon which gives us good value for money, as well as reliable service.

In view of the few years during which a 'first gun' is likely to be fully used even if it has to serve in turn two or three members of the family, a weapon of this description will meet our need for a mechanically safe gun, and especially so if it is properly looked after. However, a distinction must be drawn between a genuinely good, low-priced gun and one that merely merits the description cheap and nasty, and which, due to a combination of poor quality materials and indifferent workmanship, may become potentially unsafe after firing only a few hundred rounds even though it has in the first instance passed proof. It is hard to give any sure guidance as to how to detect such guns except to say that they are usually quite exceptionally cheap and of obscure foreign origin!

In the early days of firearms, gun barrels were often of such dubious quality, and the loading of charges so haphazard, that bursts were commonplace and frequently fatal. To rectify this state of affairs, first the Worshipful Company of Gunmakers in London, and at a later date the Guardians of the Birmingham Proof House established the London and Birmingham Proof Houses respectively, where gun barrels could be properly tested. Now by Act of Parliament all gun barrels have to be so tested, or 'pass proof' as it is known, before they can legally be offered for sale. It is an offence to sell, offer for sale, exchange or pawn any gun in this country the barrels of which have not passed proof, or are out of proof. Proof marks only show that a gun has at some time passed proof; they are not a warranty that it is still in proof, and in case of doubt with an old gun it is advisable to have a check made by a reputable gunsmith.

18.a (left) *London Proof House Provisional Proof Mark, English Make*. 18b. (right) *Birmingham Proof House Provisional Proof Mark, English Make*.

The Proof Marks are impressed on the flats of the barrels. The first such mark is one indicating the passing of Provisional Proof; the relevant ones for the London and Birmingham Proof Houses are shown in *Diagrams 18a and b* respectively. Then at a later stage the complete gun, that is with the action fitted to the barrels, is sent for a further test, and another set of marks impressed; these have altered over the years. A typical set of London and Birmingham proof marks for the years 1925-54 are shown in *Diagrams 19a and b* respectively; the ones which superseded them in 1955, and are still in force, are depicted in *Diagrams 20a and b* respectively. If a gun is sent for and passes reproof, the marks shown in *Diagrams 21a and b* are impressed. Sometimes a gun is sent for special proof, normally to ascertain that it is safe to use with a heavier load than that for which it was originally proved; the respective marks of the London and Birmingham Proof Houses are shown in *Diagrams 22a and b*.

12

NITRO PROOF 1⅛

19a. *Full proof marks 1925-1954: London*

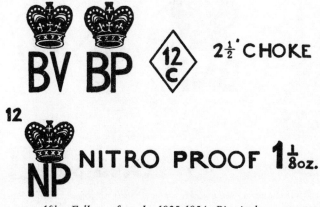

19b. *Full proof marks 1925-1954: Birmingham*

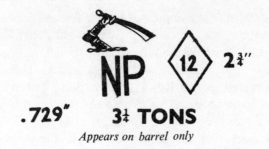

.729″   3¼ TONS

Appears on barrel only

Appears on action only

20a. *Full proof marks, since 1954, and currently in force: London (for a 2¾ in chambered gun).*

20b. *Full proof marks, since 1954, and currently in force: Birmingham (for a 2½ in chambered gun).*

21a. *London Re-proving Mark*

21b. *Birmingham Re-proving Mark.*

22a. *London Special Proof.*

22b. *Birmingham Special Proof*

Reciprocal agreements exist with the following countries whereby we accept their standards of proof and they accept ours: Austria, Belgium, Czechoslovakia, France, Italy, Spain, Southern Ireland and West Germany; but a word of warning, the pressures given in Kilograms are not directly comparable with ours in t.s.i. because they are taken at a slightly different point in the barrel, and anyway do not refer to the same thing. It is of interest that in the U.S.A. there is no official proof of firearms, so American guns offered for sale in this country must pass proof here and be marked accordingly.

Some old guns may not have the words 'Nitro Proof' stamped on the flats, which will mean they have been proved for black powder only; it is basically unsafe to use modern nitro cartridges in such a gun, and subject to the advice of a qualified gunsmith it should be immediately submitted for proof. If a gun has been fitted with new sleeved barrels each will be stamped with the word 'sleeved' on the underside in addition to the other proof marks.

These are the basic facts a young shot ought to know about proof, which is the cornerstone on which gun safety in this country has been built. For those who wish to know more, there is an excellent booklet produced by the Proof Houses jointly, entitled *Notes on The Proof of Shotguns and Other Small Arms*, which costs only a few pence and is well worth obtaining and studying.

A final point about keeping your gun in good order. Young shots are often of an enquiring turn of mind and are tempted to undertake a little exploratory surgery with a screwdriver; DON'T! I have described in the last chapter how to remove the stop pin so that the extractors can be taken out and dried; it is also permissible for anyone who can use a screwdriver efficiently, i.e. without burring the heads of the pins, to remove the locks of a sidelock after a day's shooting in the rain, so that these can be dried properly. But unless you are really prepared to learn gunsmithing under a qualified instructor, so that you will know precisely the limitations on what you can accomplish with the facilities you have at home, this is as far as the ordinary layman should go, or he will be liable to do more damage than good.

Safe gun handling and shooting in the field are largely a question of following established drills, the reasons for which if not at once obvious to a young shot should quickly become so as he gains in experience. The principal points at issue cannot be better summarized I feel than by quoting the so-called 'Golden Rules' set out in *Modern Game Shooting* in the Lonsdale Library; they are as follows:—

1. Prove if a gun is loaded or not as soon as you lay hands on it.
2. Only point a gun at quarry you wish to shoot, never at people.
3. Check that the bore/s of your gun is/are clear before you load at the beginning of a day, drive, or walk up, or after any significant interval between shots, and invariably after a misfire.
4. Never put down or leave a loaded gun.
5. Carry a gun with the barrels pointing either up in the air or down at the ground, except when you come to the 'Ready' position to take a shot, when they should point where you are looking.
6. Learn to shoot in good style; polished performance promotes safety.
7. Don't shoot where you cannot see; small shot can travel over two hundred yards before it becomes spent, and may

ricochet off stones, hard ground, water, or the branches of trees, etc.

8. Always check your gun before crossing an obstacle, or entering a car or building, and if it is loaded, unload it.

9. Don't be a greedy shot; observe proper safety angles, and never swing your muzzles through the line of guns or beaters, or any individual, such as a stop.

10. Only use cartridges which you know give ballistics within the limits for which your gun has been proved.

11. If you take a dog shooting with you, make sure it is always kept under proper control.

12. Don't take other people on trust as safe shots.

Let us now see what are the practical implications of these rules. Young people often think that the dangers of the supposedly unloaded gun are exaggerated, but from my own experience I am certain that one can never check too often that a firearm is in fact unloaded. On three occasions, once from a car and twice from a cupboard in a house, I have picked up a weapon with the owner's consent and assurance that it was not loaded, only to find on opening the breech that it was fully loaded. It is an unnerving situation, and you do not require much imagination to realize how easily an accident could have occurred if the owner had been taken at his word and the trigger pulled before the weapon was checked. So I regard it as an absolutely vital rule always to check any firearm the moment you lay hands on it, and satisfy yourself whether or not it is loaded. As a corollary to this, it should be regarded not only as a simple courtesy, but a normal safety drill, always to hand another person a firearm with the breech open, so that he can see for himself that the weapon is unloaded. If, as may sometimes be the case, this is impracticable, he should at least be shown the empty breech before it is closed, and the gun handed to him.

This leads us conveniently to the more controversial question of when it is good manners and good sense to carry a gun with the breech open, and when it may properly be carried with the breech closed. As a guide line, if the breech of a gun is open everyone, particularly anyone you are going to talk to who might in the circumstances justifiably think your gun could be loaded, can see that it is not. However, there can be situations in which a gun should be at 'instant readiness' so to speak, when it is justifiable to have the breech closed even though somebody may come along with some important information. However, I believe such occasions should be regarded as the exception that proves the rule, not invalidates it, as some 'closed breech' protagonists like to maintain. So make it a rule to carry your gun over your arm with the breech open unless circumstances genuinely dictate otherwise.

Rule 2 is only a more prosaic way of saying 'Never, never let your gun, be pointed at anyone', the force of which seems to me so indisputable that no further elaboration is necessary.

If you make it a drill to check that the bores of your gun are clear at the beginning of a day's shooting, and subsequently as indicated in Rule 3, you may well one day save yourself a burst or bulged barrel, because bits of cleaning material can easily be left in the bore from a previous day, or mud, snow or other debris become lodged in the bore while walking between beats in the course of a shooting day.

But the most deadly possibility can arise from a misfire when on opening the breech there appears to be no cartridge in the chamber; if a 20-bore cartridge is loaded by mistake into a 12-bore chamber, it can slip forward and lodge in the cone, allowing a 12-bore cartridge to be loaded on top of it so that the gun is double shotted. If the gun is then fired the pressure generated by the explosion of both cartridges is usually fierce enough to crack the action right through in the line of the face, and rip the barrel asunder in front of the breech, which may well cause the shooter the loss of one or more fingers, possibly an eye, or worse. The same contingency can occur if a 28-bore cartridge is loaded in error in a 16-bore. So if you ever have a misfire, and such is the reliability of modern British cartridges that they are a very rare event indeed, always check that the bore, not merely the chamber, is clear before you reload.

Rule 4 is really an extension of Rule 1, and its validity seems to me therefore beyond dispute.

Two correct ways of carrying a gun safely are shown in *Diagram 23a and b*. There are of course others, but do avoid ways such as depicted in *Diagram 24a and b*, in which a fellow gun or other person can find he is looking straight down your muzzles; not only are people apt to find this disturbing, but if one happens to be your host or his keeper he may make his objections plain in colourful language, which can be embarrassing, and may also

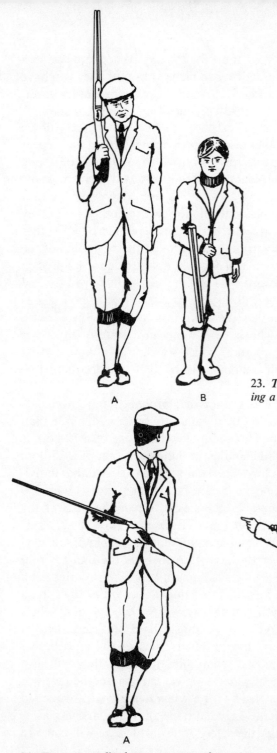

23. *Two correct ways of carrying a gun safely.*

A   B

24. *Two potentially dangerous ways of carrying a gun; that of the man, 24a, is used by a surprising number of shooting men who should know better.*

mean an end is put to your sport for the day. When you attend a driven shoot, a sound practice is to place your gun after you have unloaded it at the end of each drive in a canvas or leather cover, and carry it in this until you reach your place at the next stand.

If you watch an accomplished shot in a hot corner, you will see him mount, fire and reload his gun, pick his next target and repeat the process, all in a fluent ritual, from which any signs of undue haste or 'flap' are conspicuously absent. He will seem to know instinctively where his safe arcs of fire are, and never waste a second glance at birds outside them, however tempting a shot they may offer. In fact you are watching a 'professional' by any other name, who will have spent the spare time at the beginning of the drive working out where it will and will not be safe to shoot when birds start to come forward, and where if possible he will try and kill them. His reloading drill, footwork, etc will be as polished as he can make them. He has therefore just that little bit of extra time that the novice, who is continually in a state of fluster, is lacking. This is the standard at which we should all aim, so that we always have that vital moment in hand to decide whether or not the unexpected shot is safe.

Never shoot where you cannot see; probably more accidents occur in the shooting field due to failure to observe this rule than any other. Although the maximum effective range of a 12-bore is considered to be 45 yards, and as we have seen that of a 28-bore only 35 yards with a $\frac{1}{2}$-choke barrel, it must be realized that individual pellets of small shot (i.e. 5s, 6s, or 7s) carry on to about 250 yards before they become spent, irrespective of the bore of the gun from which they have been fired. Even at a range of 150 yards a pellet may have sufficient remaining energy to blind someone for life if it hits him in the eye. Also there is the danger from ricochets; it is surprising how comparatively few shooting men appreciate what a real menace this can be. Because of their small size, spherical shape and comparatively low velocity shot pellets can be deflected not only by obviously hard surfaces, such as stones or frozen ground, but by others such as the branches of trees, and even the quills of game bird feathers; they will also ricochet off the surface of water, so great care should be taken to ensure you have a clear field of fire when dealing with wounded duck on water, especially in conditions of semi-darkness as is often the case. Although the safety zones, which we will come to in a moment, take account of the general possibilities of ricochets, the angle through which a pellet may be deflected on ricochet is completely unpredictable, and instances have been known where it has been well over 90°. Fortunately such freak occurrences are extremely rare, and for the purpose of assessing practical danger areas we can discount them.

Special caution should be observed when shooting ground game, i.e. hares and rabbits, in cover and along hedgerows. If you can't see whether you have a clear field of fire the other side of a patch of dense cover or a hedge, don't shoot. The same applies to a pheasant flying back along the line of a hedge, or a covey of patridges scudding away low over roots, or some other crop, towards a hedge, behind which a farm worker may well be enjoying his lunch. So I say again, don't shoot where you cannot see, irrespective of whether you are having a walk round on your own with your dog, or enjoying a day's shooting in the company of others.

Rule 8 seems self-explanatory, and the danger of bringing a loaded shotgun into a dwelling obvious. But despite this, fatal accidents are reported in the daily press every year due to failure to observe this simple and seemingly self-evident rule.

It is a pleasure to see youthful enthusiasm in the shooting field, and I am all for encouraging it, providing it stops short of trying to shoot a neighbour's birds before he can. Even if it is common knowledge that old so-and-so is a palpably poor shot, it is still good manners to let him shoot first at birds rising in front of him, or coming straight to him, before you attempt to wipe his eye! But quite apart from this, greedy shooting almost invariably leads to dangerous shooting, and should not be countenanced. The safety angles and zones you should observe are set out in *Diagram 25*. Although a line of guns has been depicted, the same angles should apply if you are a walking gun in a line of beaters, and in relation to any individual person, such as a stop or picker up, or someone not connected with your shooting at all, such as a farm worker. Say you are walking in line at a rough shoot, and having just killed in front with your right barrel, you wish to turn for a shot at a rabbit behind the line; the correct procedure is for you to bring the stock down from your shoulder, so that the muzzles point straight up in the air as the gun swings past the other people in the line; then as you complete your turn you remount the gun

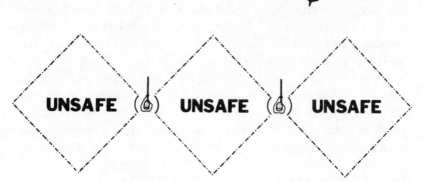

25. *The safety angles you should observe in relation to all other people in the shooting field, not only fellow guns.*

and shoot. (See *Diagram 26*.) Even if only a single person is involved, you should always follow the same drill. Referring back to *Diagram 25*, neither ground game nor low birds should be shot in the shaded danger zones, though reasonably high birds can be, provided you are shooting at an angle of at least 45° in the vertical plane, but even then it is good manners not to shoot birds directly over your neighbour's head.

The importance of only using cartridges which give ballistics within the limits for which your gun has been proved has already been discussed. British cartridges have marked on the box the guns for which they are suitable. With some brands of foreign cartridges, this information is not always clear; in any case of doubt it is advisable to consult a qualified gunsmith before using them, or you may damage both your gun and yourself.

For many shooting men a great deal of the pleasure they obtain from their sport derives from the handling and working of their dog. This is fine provided the dog in question is reasonably well trained and steady. A dog that is not under proper control is more than merely a nuisance, it is a potential menace to safety in a variety of ways. In particular I dislike seeing people out shooting with dogs attached to their belts by a lead. If a sizeable Labrador plunges forward just as its owner is in the middle of taking a shot, the latter will be thrown off balance, and the charge may go anywhere. So if you want to shoot with a dog, which in my view is

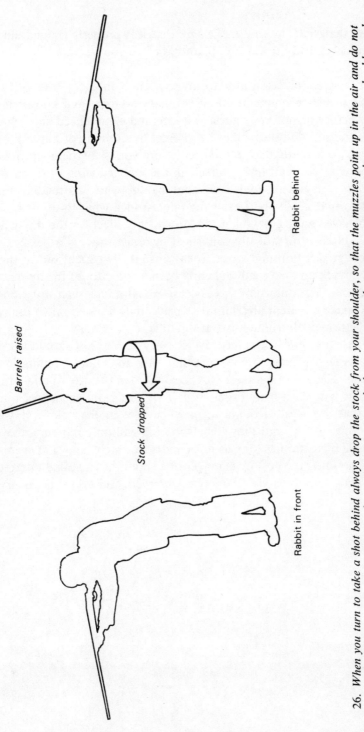

Barrels raised

Stock dropped

Rabbit behind

Rabbit in front

26. *When you turn to take a shot behind always drop the stock from your shoulder, so that the muzzles point up in the air and do not 'cover' a neighbouring gun or anyone else as you swing round; then as you complete your turn, remount the gun to your shoulder and fire.*

59

more than half the fun, make sure that it is properly trained, and genuinely steady to fur and feather, before you venture with it in the field.

It is splendid being able to invite a guest to a day's shooting. But I would recommend that if you have no first hand knowledge of whether or not your guest is a safe and experienced shot, you take steps to find out, either by discreet questioning of himself, or by asking a mutual acquaintance, before you issue the invitation. Otherwise you can find yourself in the embarrassing position of having a complete novice on your hands, who is attending his first formal shoot and hasn't the faintest idea what to do or how to behave; your growing suspicions to this effect on the day will probably be dramatically confirmed by a near-miss at a beater or fellow gun, if nothing worse! I was once badly caught out in this way myself and have subsequently been a spectator of the discomfiture of others on two or three occasions. Although such situations may make excellent after-dinner stories, they are seldom so funny to the principal protagonists at the time.

These are the basic safety 'drills' every young shot should learn and perfect, if he is to become a safe shot and enjoy a reputation as one. There is of course a great deal more in the way of etiquette that he will learn from experience. Two important aspects of this are that the word of the host, or whoever is in charge of a day's shooting, is law, and that game shooting will only remain an enjoyable recreation as long as it is conducted safely, and that everyone, not only the host or manager of a shoot, has a vested interest in seeing that the code of safety is observed, and also if necessary enforced.

Chapter VI

How to shoot your best

We have dealt with the questions of what sort of gun you should have, why and how it ought to fit you, what cartridge it should be matched with to obtain the best results, and what you should do in order to shoot safely with it. We can now turn to the final problem, how to shoot successfully with it.

It used to be thought that good game shots were born and could not be made. This is nonsense. As with any other recreation, becoming a competent performer is for the majority simply a matter of learning from a capable instructor. This is not to suggest that some will not prove more adept pupils than others. But given the right tuition only a tiny majority should prove incurable duffers. Happily game shooting is not a competitive sport, but neither is fox hunting, yet the virtue of being a good horseman is universally acknowledged, and most people take pride in trying to become one and obtain the best instruction they can to this end. So let the young shot set out to become as good a marksman as he can; it will ensure a minimum of suffering to live quarry he subsequently pursues, so he can properly consider it very much a part of becoming a good sportsman.

Shooting schools are still comparatively few and far between, but the aspiring young game shot cannot do better than attend one right from the start of his shooting career. However, it should be realized that some instructors favour one style, others another, which can mean the measurements given by 'A' for stock length, cast off, etc may vary from those supplied by 'B'. So it is worth taking the trouble to find an instructor in whom you really have confidence, and to persevere with him, because if you chop and change, you will no sooner have settled into one style than you will be altering it in favour of another to the detriment of your general progress.

There are basically two methods of shooting moving targets with a shotgun; the swing and intercept method in which the gun is swung through the target and discharged at a point in space ahead of it where it is anticipated the shot will hit it, and the instinctive method in which you shoot apparently at the target and rely on 'overthrow' to ensure the shot hits it. The former is in theory the obvious way of tackling a moving target and has been recognized as such since the days of bows and arrows. However, it depends for its success on ability to estimate correctly the necessary lead or forward allowance, and this, as anti-aircraft gunners have discovered in more modern times, is its great weakness in practice. Certainly in game shooting, where every shootable target in the course of a day will probably be travelling at a different height, speed and angle, altogether too much guesswork becomes involved to ensure consistently successful results, So it is the latter method that I propose to deal with hereunder and which I believe once mastered will enable a young shot to shoot to the best of his natural ability all the time.

As with games and other sports, successful game shooting is mainly a matter of good coordination of hand and eye, aided by good footwork. So let us deal with each of these in turn, starting with the feet. I shall be referring throughout this chapter to the right-handed shot, so those who shoot left-handed should transpose right for left and vice versa.

Correct positioning and use of the feet should enable you to shoot with equal facility at quarry approaching or departing from any point of the compass, subject of course to limits imposed by any danger zones. There may be times, such as when you are kneeling in a gutter out wildfowling, that you find you can shoot remarkably well without benefit of footwork; don't let these mislead you into thinking it is therefore of little account. The agility and suppleness of young people can often overcome deficiencies in footwork, but as you grow older and stiffen these will increasingly handicap you. So set out from the start to learn how to use your feet correctly, then when the time arrives when you find there is no substitute for good footwork, it will with luck have become an instinctive part of your shooting 'drill'.

Beginners are sometimes influenced by pictures they have seen of soldiers in the 'standing firing' position, with the left foot well advanced in front of the right. Forget all about this; game shots do not have to repel charges by cavalry or primitive tribesmen! You should stand rather square to your front with your feet positioned as in *Diagram 27*, that is with the right foot slightly withdrawn, and the heels 2-4 in apart, depending on your height. If you are very tall, say over 6 ft, you may need a slightly wider stance. The real criterion is that with the weight balanced equally on both feet, it should feel comfortable and right. Avoid adopting a wider stance, because it will impede your ability to turn and may mean you are off balance when you do.

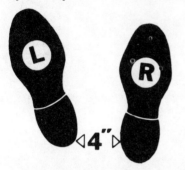

27. *The correct position of the feet; whilst awaiting a shot the weight should be equally balanced on both.*

If you wish to shoot a target to your left, you should transfer the weight to your left foot as you start to turn at the hips. As the angle of your turn increases, the right heel should begin to rise, and the right foot to pivot about the toe. A normally supple adult, should find he can turn through an arc of well over 90° quite easily in this way, so a young shot certainly should experience no difficulty. A similar procedure should be adopted for dealing with a target to the right, only this time the weight is put on the right foot, and it is the left heel that rises with the increasing angle of turn, and the left toe that is the pivot. (See *Diagrams 28a and b*.) Most of us find the turn to the left comes quite fluently and naturally, but with that to the right some people forget to raise the left heel, and so stand 'flat-footed'. As a result the angle of turn they can achieve is restricted, and in order to increase it they bend over at the waist. This causes their gun muzzles to travel in an arc instead of in a straight line along the flight path of their target, and their shot goes low in consequence; this is known as 'rainbowing' and is depicted in *Diagram 29*.

A   B

28. *When turning to shoot to the left or right, the right or left heel respectively must be raised as the angle of turn increases.*

RAINBOWING

29. *If a shooter stands 'flat-footed' when he turns to take a shot, he will have to bend at the waist, causing his shoulder to drop and the gun barrels to cant; as a result he will shoot low and behind.*

With a shot low in front, you should place the weight on your front, or left foot, and as you lean forward into your shot, the heel of the right foot should rise (see *Diagram 30*.) Similarly with a high overhead shot the weight should flow smoothly back on to the right foot, and the left heel be raised to allow the backswing to carry on unchecked to the maximum limit (see *Diagram 31*.)

Right heel raised

Left heel on ground

30. *As you lean forward to take a shot low in front with the weight going on to your left foot, your right heel should rise.*

Follow through

Left heel raised

31. *As you bring the weight back on to your right leg to take a high overhead shot, the left heel should rise.*

These are the basic elements of good footwork. As with games, practice makes perfect, so take your gun and a couple of 'snap caps', (dummy rounds) and put in a bit of 'dry' practice at these turns, etc in the garden. Remember the locks of a shotgun should never be 'fired' on an empty chamber, so make sure you acquire two snap caps for this and other 'dry' practice.

E

Now we come to the positioning of the hands and their role. Each hand has two functions; both should contribute equally to the lifting and moving of the gun; additionally, the left hand has to direct the muzzles on to the target and the right to operate the triggers. The right hand should grip the small of the butt, or 'hand' as it is called, as shown in *Diagram 32*. It will be seen that the right forefinger should be laid along the trigger guard, while the side of the thumb rests against the rear of the safety catch, so that it can readily push it forward as the gun is mounted to the shoulder for a shot. It is important that the top of the thumb should not be used to shove the safety catch forward, or on recoil after firing the sharp end of the top lever may split or badly bruise the shooter's thumb. The left hand should grasp the barrels in the region of the top of the fore-end, as illustrated in *Diagram 33*. It will be noted that the left thumb points straight down the side of the left barrel, and so the muzzles will be aimed exactly where the shooter's left thumb is pointing; the other important feature is that the tips of the fingers of the left hand do not encroach over the top of the right barrel, so that the top rib remains the eye-catching centreline of the barrels, the importance of which will be explained in a moment.

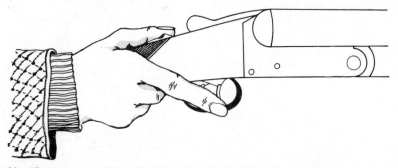

32. *The correct right hand hold in the 'Ready' position, as you await a shot.*

So much for the actual hand holds; the importance of the gun being correctly mounted to the shoulder for each shot has already been mentioned in Chapter III. Accuracy in this respect is greatly assisted if the stock has only to be moved a short distance to the shoulder. As soon as a shot is anticipated a shooter should therefore assume the 'Ready Position' depicted in *Diagram 34*. In this

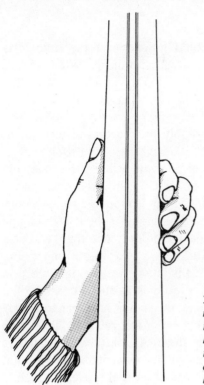

33. The correct left hand hold in the region of the top of the fore-end; note the thumb pointing straight down the left side of the barrels, and the finger tips gripping the right side, so as not to encroach over the top of the right barrel.

34. The 'Ready' position with the stock tucked under the armpit, and the muzzles pointing where the shooter is looking.

it will be seen that the end of the butt is tucked up under the shooter's armpit so that it is squeezed gently but firmly between his upper arm and ribs. The hands are positioned as already described, and the muzzles should point where the shooter is looking ·in expectation of his target appearing. What should happen next, when the gun is mounted to the shoulder, is so closely involved with the part played by the eyes, that we will deal with it in conjunction with them.

The human eyes are a remarkably precise optical instrument and if we regard them as such, working in conjunction with a computer, namely the brain, that controls a firing lever, i.e. the trigger finger, we shall readily understand how the principle of 'overthrow' works in practice. If the gun is mounted to the shoulder from the 'ready position', and the moment the muzzles come to bear on the target, the eyes give the order to fire, there will be a momentary delay while the brain activates the trigger finger, and the trigger is actually pulled. This is known as 'personal reaction time' and in a normal healthy person is about a quarter of a second (.25 secs). If the action of the hands has been properly synchronized with that of the eyes, the muzzles will have been accelerating past the target when the eyes gave their order to fire and in this brief interval of .25 secs will have swept ahead to a point that enables the shot to hit the target in flight, even though it appeared to the shooter that he fired directly at his target.

There are several other matters related to this that the shooter should also understand if he is to comprehend fully why this method of instictive shooting works in practice and is not just a form of snap-shooting, as is sometimes wrongly suggested. It relies entirely on the shooter trusting his eye, and as in golf, squash or cricket, keeping his eye on the ball, or in this case having eyes for nothing but the target. This means he must no more consciously look at his gun barrels as he shoots than a golfer would look at the head of his club as he strikes the ball or a cricketer the blade of his bat. He must rely on his hands doing instinctively what is needful, so that if his feet and everything else are properly coordinated, he will score a hit, just as does a golfer or cricketer. All accurate shooting by manual means, be it with a bow and arrow or anything else, depends on the shooter having a recognizable and consistent aiming mark to use as a datum point from which adjustments can be made in the event of a miss. This requirement is met if the target itself, or a particular part of it, forms the point of aim. It is certainly not met by indeterminate points in space ahead of, or elsewhere in relation to, the target, as required in the swing and intercept method.

If the human eye sees something generally which has width or length, it will automatically register the centre of it, unless it is consciously directed to a particular part. Thus when a pair of gun barrels enter a shooter's field of vision, although he continues to look steadfastly at his target, his eyes will take note of their centre line. This is why it is so important not to obscure part of the right barrel with the fingers of the left hand, because it creates a false centreline somewhere down the left barrel, which can induce an error of aim. It is also the reason why with a target that has length, such as a direct crossing pheasant, the shooter must fix his eyes on the head, or they will focus on the middle, and a tailed or missed bird will be the outcome.

In game shooting both eyes are normally used, because binocular vision enables range to be judged, whereas monocular vision does not.

There is one further matter relating to the eyes; sooner or later a young shot is bound to hear the 'Master Eye' concept mentioned. With right-handed people their right arm is generally stronger and more used than their left, though the degree to which the right arm is favoured can vary quite substantially from those whose left hand is always used in a subsidiary capacity, to others who are almost equally at home with it as their right. As a right-handed person is also usually right-footed, that is his right leg is the stronger, it seems logical to assume that he will also generally be right-eyed, in other words his right eye will be the dominant, or 'master eye', of the two and exert the greater influence over his line of sight. In fact when this theory is applied in gun-fitting in ascertaining cast-off, this is usually found to be the case. Some people see fit to ridicule the master eye concept, but I have yet to find a critic able to propound a better one which will work in practice.

The head should be held fairly upright so that the eyes are level; a bird's-eye view of a shooter with a properly fitted gun is shown in *Diagram 35*, from which it will be seen that both the eyes and gun muzzles are looking straight at the target.

Let us now go through the drill for actually taking a shot. As soon as you anticipate the appearance of a target within range, you should take up the ready position. Then when it comes into view, or just before it arrives within range if it is already in view,

35. *A target's eye view of a shooter when his gun fits him, and has been correctly mounted to the shoulder.*

you should fix your eyes on it; at the same time the hands should direct the muzzles on to it, and keep them there, the stock remaining tucked under your arm. Once you have thus 'addressed' your target, to borrow a golfing expression, you must not move your head independently of your body until after you have completed your shot; in other words you must remain 'stiff necked'. As soon as you reckon the moment has arrived to take your shot, move the gun forward from under your arm, thumbing off the safety catch as you do so; continue the movement by bringing the gun smoothly but smartly up into the shoulder, so that as the butt beds home there, the muzzles bear on the target, your eyes give the order to fire, and your finger pulls the trigger. It is fatal to dwell on the aim; you must trust your eyes and pull the trigger when they 'tell' you. If by chance you do not fire, return to the ready position and reapply the safety catch.

It is most important that the movement of the gun from under the arm up into the shoulder is briskly executed in one fluent movement because it provides the impulsion that produces the overthrow on which success depends. If you start to mount the gun too soon, the movement will lose its vital spontaneity, become artificially prolonged and in the final instance be completely lacking in the essential impulsion, so that a miss behind becomes inevitable. In fact premature gun mounting is a common cause of missing, notably where targets come into view an appreciable time before they arrive within range, such as in the case of woodpigeon flighting to their woodland roosts of a winter's evening, or driven pheasants.

The late Robert Churchill used to reckon that head movement during gun mounting was one of the commonest causes of missing. A frequent manifestation of this with young shots is bobbing the head down to meet the stock. This can certainly be provoked by too long a stock, but sometimes even if it is the right length, over-eagerness in trying to get their shots off can cause novices to fall into the habit, particularly if they are doing a lot of shooting at ground game, or woodpigeon coming in low to decoys. The stock must always be brought up to the cheek. So if this fault is detected, bring out the snap caps again and take a series of 'dry' shots at the reflection of your own eye in a mirror; you will soon be able to check if you are bobbing your head down.

If you carry out the drill outlined above, trust your eye, and shoot spontaneously at your targets, you should kill every time. But even the best shots have their misses, so when you do, don't become unduly disheartened or worried. Go back over your drill, and think where you may have gone wrong. Are you trying too hard and taking a quick squint down the barrels to make sure they are on target? This will mean you have been taking your eye off the 'ball' just at the critical moment before you pull the trigger, which can have a disastrous effect on your shooting, as it would on your cricket if you switched your gaze from ball to bat just before striking the former.

Finally, I have said before, and make no apology for saying again, get as much shooting practice as you can. The right way to do this is at clays; otherwise you will cause unnecessary suffering, which is not good sportsmanship. You may hear some people say that shooting at clays is bad for your game shooting because a clay is slowing up whereas a game bird is accelerating. This is a fallacy. Game birds are by no means always accelerating in flight, and certainly many woodpigeon you shoot over decoys will not be. But whether your target is accelerating or decelerating is really immaterial, it will still give you practice in coordination of hands and eyes, which is what it is all about. However, different quarry do require different timing, and just as a cricketer has to adjust from fast bowling to slow, and may take an over or two to do so, you will find if you go straight from high clays at a shooting ground to the 'bolted rabbit' stand, it will take you a few shots to adjust to the different circumstances and timing, or in other words to get your eye in again.

Now let us move on and see what special problems are posed by some of the quarry we are likely to shoot in the field.

Chapter VII

Shooting in the field

When you have mastered the elements of shooting by practice at clays, you will be eager to try your skill in the field. But before you do so there are one or two points of difference which it will help you to understand. Unlike the clays which were presented so as to give you a fair chance of hitting them, many of the quarry you pursue, particularly woodpigeon and rabbits, will, as soon as they are aware of your presence, take evasive action to make it as difficult as possible for you to hit them. So even if you make the most of your opportunities out shooting you cannot expect to achieve the same degree of success as you did with clays. Thus if, for example, you have been able to break eight out of ten clays with your first barrel fairly regularly, do not be dismayed if in the field you only manage to account for four quarry with ten shots, because you will probably have been shooting very creditably. To put the matter in perspective, Sir Ralph Payne-Gallwey, who was one of the great game shots in this country around the beginning of the century, reckoned that over the course of a whole season, a sportsman who made the most of his chances (i.e. he did not just pick the easy shots and ignore the difficult ones!) would qualify as a good marksman if he averaged 35 head in the bag for every 100 cartridges fired. This would mean that on some days he would do better than this, and on others not so well. The complete table of Sir Ralph's assessment of marksmanship is given overleaf.

This table is included so that you can work out quietly for yourself whether or not you have reason to be satisfied with your own performance. There is no more tiresome companion on a shooting day than someone who is continually fussing about his 'average' of kills to cartridges and keeps telling everyone else how well or badly he is doing! Game shooting is not a competitive sport, so shoot away to the best of your ability and enjoy yourself.

Inferior Marksman	..	..	25 kills per 100 cartridges
Average Marksman	..	..	30 „ „ „ „
Good Marksman	..	..	35 „ „ „ „
Very Good Marksman		..	40 „ „ „ „
First Class Marksman		..	45 „ „ „ „

Your clays were always projected so that you could 'kill' them within range. Game and other quarry will usually be doing its best to get out of range and stay there. So to avoid unnecessary wounding you must be aware of the limits at which you can shoot. Unfortunately it is difficult to give sound practical guidance on how to estimate ranges, the ability to do so being largely acquired by experience, and even then one can on occasion find oneself seriously at fault. However, I have found the following measures of help. You should have a mental picture of what the maximum effective range of your gun looks like on the ground. In the case of a 28-bore this will be 30-35 yards, so pace out 35 yards in the garden, put down a marker such as a rubber pigeon decoy, return to your starting point and have a good, long look at it. Note how it looks for size, how clearly the white collar shows up, or any other distinguishing features. Follow this up next time you exercise the dog, or go for a walk in the country, by estimating and then pacing out the distance to a gate post, a bale of straw, a tree, or any other prominent mark. If you make a habit of doing this when you are out for a walk, you should soon find you are able to estimate 'targets' at ranges of between 20 and 35 yards quite accurately.

Estimating the height of quarry on the wing is a rather more difficult problem. But again it is a help to have a datum line from which to work. The average two-storey house with a pitch roof is about 30 ft high; if on a country walk you come across a fallen tree, pace out its length, and you will find a typical tall tree in a shelter belt or woodland is around 60 ft. If you come across a stand of really high beeches, and one has been blown down so that you can pace out its length, it may well measure 100 ft, but trees of such a height are exceptional. Then spend a little while whenever you can, just watching the birds, whatever they may be, flying over such a house or trees, and train your eye to judge if they are as high again, half as high again, or only just skimming the tops. You will then be able to say to yourself: That bird is about 60 or 90 ft high, or as the case may be, and so either would or would not be in shot if I was a waiting gun.

If you train your eyes to estimate ranges on the ground and in the air in some such ways it will help you to avoid taking shots at excessive range, which is not only unsporting but can be most annoying to your companions because it may well put other game afoot or on the wing out of range.

But so much for generalities, let us now have a look at some particular cases. Wherever you go in the British countryside you are bound to come across the ubiquitous woodpigeon. They are rated as a pest so there is no close season, but they can provide magnificent sport and are excellent eating if cooked properly. However, they can prove most elusive targets. This is not because they can 'take a lot of shot' as some people assert, for they are just as vulnerable to a properly centred pattern of No. 7s as any other quarry you will shoot, nor because they are specially fast flyers, for they are not, but because they have astonishing powers of acceleration and manoeuvrability which they will bring into play if they see you before you shoot. So, whenever you are lying in wait for woodpigeon you must keep absolutely still until you raise your gun to fire.

The two principal ways of shooting them are over decoys set up in a crop off which they are feeding and as they flight into woods to roost of a winter's evening, sometimes in flocks numbering hundreds. Great sport can be had with decoys chiefly in the months of March to October, though given favourable conditions success may be achieved at any time of year; flighting them is really a winter sport after the leaf is off the trees, from December to March. There is a great deal more to both decoying and flighting than just the actual shooting involved, but lack of space prohibits a description here. I can but recommend the reader who wants to learn more to study the relevant chapter in *Modern Game Shooting* in the Lonsdale Library.

However, casual encounters with woodpigeon in the course of a walk with a gun round a shoot can also give good sport. If you walk quietly down a field alongside a rather overgrown hedgerow, or along the outside of a woodland or shelter belt, it will only be a matter of time before you hear the unmistakable clatter of a

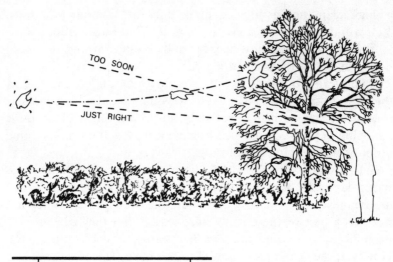

TOO SOON

JUST RIGHT

| 25-30 yards | 10-15 yards |

36. *A woodpigeon often swoops downwards instead of upwards when it breaks cover. Pause a moment before shooting. Bring your gun to the ready position, and fix your eyes on the target. Then take your shot. If you mount your gun smartly and correctly, you should kill every time.*

woodie thrashing its way out of a bush or tree. This should give you time to come to the ready position in anticipation of its appearance in the open, very possibly only a few yards ahead of you. Generally as soon as the bird has cleared cover, it will set off as fast as its wings can carry it, pursuing a slightly downward path in order to gain speed quickly. If in the excitement of the moment, you straightway whirl up your gun and shoot, not only is it likely to be too close, but you will almost certainly shoot over the top of it. (see *Diagram 36*) Instead, pause for a moment, fix your eyes on the bird so they have a chance to assess the line of flight correctly, then shoot. If you have mounted your gun properly you should have made a first barrel kill at 25-30 yards range. (see again *Diagram 36*) By pausing for that fraction of a second to give your eyes a better chance, you will also have gained the advantage of a bigger lethal pattern than you would have obtained at closer quarters. So when any quarry flushes near by, don't rush your shot.

Another typical encounter with woodpigeon in the course of a walk round is the bird that departs from the topmost branches of a tree and is going directly away from you. This is not a difficult shot, but it does require a slight modification of the technique described in the last chapter, in that you will appear to shoot a little ahead of your target without the muzzles ever having come to bear on it. But once again trust your eyes, they will not let you down.

Woodpigeon can probably offer a wider variety of shots than any other quarry, so they provide splendid advanced training for a young shot and he should grasp every opportunity of going pigeon shooting that comes his way. When he can justly claim to be able to kill one bird to every three cartridges, he will indeed be able to consider himself a marksman in the making.

With the resurgence of rabbit populations, the possibility of a young shot being able to enjoy some good sport with rabbits has greatly improved. They do not offer such challenging shooting as woodpigeon, but despite this the ability to bowl them head over heels regularly does call for a definite skill. With a direct going away shot, you must fix your eyes well up between their ears if you are to accomplish this, otherwise you will merely hit them in the hindquarters. With a direct crossing shot, remember a full grown rabbit is about 15 in long and so has significant length; you should therefore not just look at your target generally but direct your glance to its head.

Rabbits in cover can prove very tricky targets until you have mastered the knack of dealing with them. When you first encounter a rabbit bouncing away between the hazel stools like a rubber ball, it is all too easy to put the gun to one's shoulder, then dither over which gap to shoot it in and as a result miss handsomely with both barrels. Don't be put off by its appearances and disappearances amongst the patchwork of cover. Treat it as if it was in view the whole time and, if once again you trust your eye, success should be your reward. But one point you must never forget in this type of shooting is that safety must be given paramount priority, or somebody, or their dog, will get hurt.

Sometimes if you are walking along the edge of a wood in the late afternoon and, before turning the next corner, you peer cautiously round, you may spot a rabbit out feeding in the field. When dealing with a stationary target such as this, you should aim to shoot the ground from under it, or your charge will go over the top of it. (see *Diagram 37*) The same is also necessary with direct crossing shots at ground game, especially downhill.

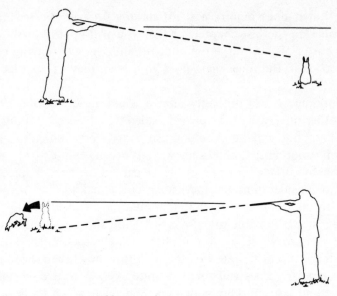

37. To hit a stationary rabbit, or other such target, you must 'aim' to shoot the ground from under it.

Generally, what has been said above about the shooting of rabbits applies with even greater force to hares. The hare is a much bigger animal, being around 24 in in length and weighing on average 8 lbs. In my experience if you can really look a hare in the eye, it will be about 30 yards distant, so with your 28-bore and a standard load of No. 6 shot you should be able to kill it cleanly if it offers you an approaching or crossing shot. However, until you have gained some experience of shooting hares, I would recommend that you do not attempt direct going away shots, as a hare's rump features so largely that it is extremely difficult .to make a clean kill. A wounded hare trailing a broken leg and limping away to die is a pitiable sight. Finally, do be particularly careful not to shoot at hares at excessive range.

Sad to say, partridges continue to decline rather than increase in numbers, and only rarely will a young shot be able to look forward to walking the stubbles and roots in September in pursuit of them. However, if and when you do, you will want to know how to deal with them. When your first covey flushes in front of you it is a very exciting moment and the air seems so full of the little brown birds that all you need do is put up your gun, pull the triggers, and at least two or three must fall as dead as door nails! Yet if you do this and 'brown' the covey, as it is known, you will almost certainly hit nothing and the covey will sail serenely on its way without the loss of a feather. The first thing you must learn with partridges, whether you are walking them up or having them driven to you, is to pick your bird as soon as the covey appears, and have eyes for none other until it crumples in the air. Many chances at partridges are muffed by switching targets.

Another cardinal rule in partridge shooting, and especially when you are walking up, is to keep as quiet as you can, and avoid all unnecessary chatter, or your hopes of getting within range of the coveys will be dashed.

Patridges are essentially low flying birds, and when driven will often appear to be coming at you rather like cricket balls on wings, giving a great impression of speed. You will be told, therefore, to take your first bird well out, which in your case with a 28-bore will mean at 30 yards, though with a 12-bore it is 40. So while waiting for a covey to come forward you should try and form a mental picture of a line on the ground 30 yards away over which you should kill your first bird. The purpose of taking this first one well out is to enable you to shoot a second in front with your left barrel. But to do this is pretty shooting which calls for skill and experience; to begin with you should be content to kill one in front, then, taking the stock down from your shoulder, turn, and shoot your second bird behind. (see *Diagram 38*) As you began to turn you should have picked out your second target, so that the moment you have faced about you are ready to shoot. Then, if fortune smiles on you, and you have executed your drill correctly, you may have brought off your first right and left! But remember this; more rights and lefts are bungled by a shooter switching his eyes from the first bird before it is killed to the one he intends to shoot next than probably any other cause.

Because of the impression of speed given by driven partridges, you will often hear it said that they need 'quick shooting'. In my opinion this is a bad way of expressing it; if you have a first barrel miss, there is no point in compounding it by immediately discharging the second, and so wasting two cartridges instead of one. What driven partridges do really call for is incisive, accurate shooting, which is a matter of picking your target, concentrating on it as hard as you can and trusting your eye when it indicates the moment has come to pull the trigger. Driven partridges are

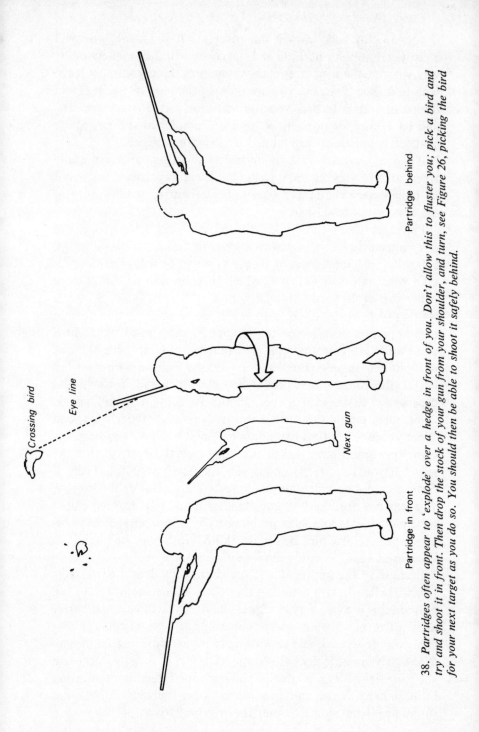

Crossing bird

Eye line

Next gun

Partridge in front

Partridge behind

38. Partridges often appear to 'explode' over a hedge in front of you. Don't allow this to fluster you; pick a bird and try and shoot it in front. Then drop the stock of your gun from your shoulder, and turn, see Figure 26, picking the bird for your next target as you do so. You should then be able to shoot it safely behind.

more often missed in front than most people realize; if you have a series of unaccountable misses try shooting the legs off the next one, and it may surprise you by crumpling in the air.

Probably the first milestone in his shooting career to which an aspiring young game shot most looks forward is the day he can proudly return home with his first cock pheasant. To many this bird must seem such a large, colourful fellow, that when flushed near at hand from roots or other low cover, he will be almost impossible to miss. Yet he not infrequently is, by novice and veteran alike. There are two main reasons for this; the commotion a cock pheasant makes as it clatters clear of cover momentarily flusters the shooter, and causes him to over-react and shoot too soon; on a dry day, once on the wing, the bird makes a remarkably quick getaway, at the start of which it climbs steeply, and as a result the over-eager gun shoots under it. Realizing this, but not that his target has now started to level out in flight, he gives his gun a mighty heave, and in consequence misses above and behind with his second barrel. The sequence of events is depicted in *Diagram 39*, as is how to deal correctly with this situation. With a bird

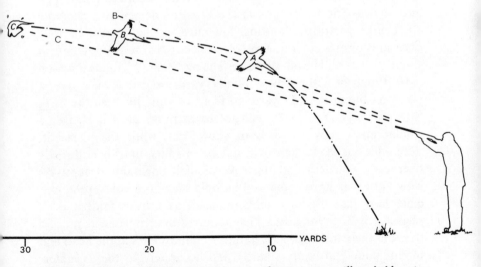

39. *If you shoot too soon at a going away pheasant, you will probably miss under it with your first barrel (shot A), and over it with your second (shot B). Follow the same drill as for the woodpigeon (Figure 36); pause, bring your gun to the ready position, and fix your eyes on your target. Then take your shot at 25-30 yards (shot C).*

flushing only a few feet or yards in front of you, you have plenty of time. First, as far as the ground allows, adopt a correct stance, at the same time bringing your gun to the ready position, and fastening your eyes on the target. When the bird has gained height and levelled out in flight, say at a distance of 20-25 yards from you, then is the time to mount your gun and shoot. If by chance you miss, which you shouldn't, you will have plenty of time for a face-saving second barrel.

A pheasant flushed from a hedgerow will often fly away low along the line of the hedge. In this case, provided it is a safe shot, you should treat it just like a going away partridge, but remember a pheasant is the faster flyer of the two, and because of its length (a cock pheasant in full plumage may be 32 in long) it is vital that you fasten your eyes on its head, not its rump, if you are to kill it cleanly.

Although it will probably be a while before you take your place in the line at a day's covert shooting, you may well during a walk round get a shot at what is tantamount to a driven bird, so you should know how to deal with it. In the majority of spinneys and woodlands trees much over 60 ft in height are exceptional and many people will tell you a pheasant at that height is a good, high bird anyway! So let us look at the situation depicted in *Diagram 40*. Unlike partridge shooting you must let high birds, be they pheasants or any other quarry, come well in before you attempt to shoot, or they will be out of range. The pheasant, 'P', in the diagram is 60 ft high; it will not be within 30 yards range until it is over a point on the ground 22 yards in front of you; likewise the bird, 'P1', which is 75 ft high, will not be in range until it is over a similar mark only 17 yards to your front, while the pheasant, 'P2', which is 90 ft high, will not be in range until it is directly overhead. You will find the pace of high pheasants deceptively slow until they have come well in, only then does your eye appreciate how fast they are moving; also, as I have said, a cock pheasant is 32 in long, of which about 18 in comprises its tail. So to shoot these tall birds successfully you must look at the head and mount your gun really smartly and accurately to the shoulder; avoid at all costs falling into the trap of mounting it prematurely. If you follow these two precepts and otherwise carry out your 'drill' correctly there is no reason why you should not shoot these high pheasants successfully with your 28-bore, possibly to the

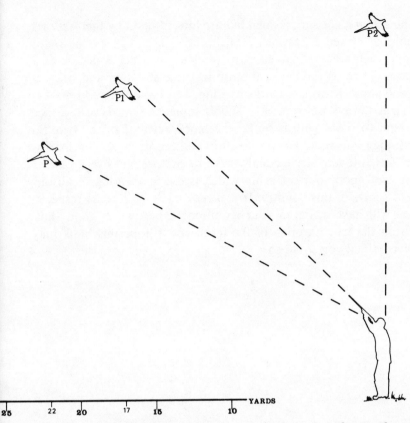

| | | | | | | YARDS |
| 25 | 22 | 20 | 17 | 15 | 10 | |

40. *You must allow all high birds to come well in before you shoot or they will be out of range. The pheasant depicted at 'P' is 60 ft high, and will not be within 30 yards range until it is over a point 22 yards in front of you on the ground. Similarly the bird at 'P1' which is 75 ft high, will need to be only 17 yards away, whilst that at 'P2', which is 90 ft high, should be shot almost directly overhead.*

surprise of older sportsmen!

There are of course many other quarry which may come your way; a young friend of mine shot his first woodcock with his 28-bore the first time out as a guest gun with the aplomb of a veteran. You may be fortunate enough to get an occasional shot at wild duck; but be careful when you do on two counts; mallard are heavily plumaged birds, and many shooting men would regard even No. 6 shot as being on the light side, so you must hit them well forward to ensure a clean kill; secondly they will quickly climb out of range on a calm day, so if they circle back over you after they have, don't be tempted into taking a shot.

You will find as you gain experience that there are some people who are first class marksmen but are looked upon by their fellows more as 'hired assassins', while others, although perhaps not quite such crack shots, seem to receive a warmer welcome at a shoot. There is a great deal more to game shooting and being a 'good shot' than mere marksmanship, and though a good marksman is always welcome at a shoot, someone who is also a nice person to shoot with is by far the more welcome of the two. So although you should spare no effort to become as good a marksman as you can, strive equally hard to capture and live up to the spirit of good sportsmanship which is the mainspring of all our field sports in this country. If you succeed in both these respects, you will have achieved your ambition to become a 'good shot' within the true meaning of the term, and I hope this book may have helped you to do so.

Index